The Lolo Trail
by
Ralph S. Space

Second Edition
HISTORIC MONTANA PUBLISHING
MISSOULA, MONTANA, 2001

Dedicated to Shaun Lea—
who teaches the primacy of love

All photos by JJSmith unless otherwise noted.
Printed on recycled paper.

Other books by Historic Montana Publishing:
Hanging the Sheriff: A Biography of Henry Plummer by R.E. Mather and F.E. Boswell
The Montana History Calendar by Jeffrey J. Smith

Library of Congress Cataloging-in-Publication Data

Space, Ralph S.
   The Lolo Trail: a history and a guide to the trail of Lewis and Clark / by Ralph S. Space.–2nd ed.
      p. cm.
  Includes bibliographical references and index.
  ISBN 0-9663355-2-X
   1. Bird-Traux (Idaho and Mont.)–History. 2. Bird-Traux Trail (Idaho and Mont.)–Guidebooks. 3. Lewis and Clark Expedition (1804-1806) I. Title.

F752.B64 S64 2001
917.804'2–dc21   2001016706

Printed in Canada

CONTENTS

Ralph S. Space's Introduction to his 1970 Edition

I have here attempted to combine all these historical events in one book. I have also added an experience of my own that I believe is interesting.

I first crossed the Lolo Trail in 1924 when it was a horse trail. Since it was converted into a road over 35 years ago, those who traveled it as a trail are all old and becoming fewer in number each year. I, therefore, present the story of the Lolo Trail as one who traveled it as historical parties did before it was made easy by construction of a road.

Acknowledgment

Thanks to Judy Space for her great generosity in letting me republish her late father's book. I would also like to say how deeply honored I am by Josiah Blackeagle Pinkham's welcome, Stephen Ambrose's preface, and Bud Moore's introduction to this edition of *The Lolo Trail*. Thanks also to Wayne and Gia Fairchild, Roman Kuczer, Chris Autio, Bruce Truett, Bob Doty, Frank Costanza, Chris Partridge, Cheri Jones, C. Milo McLeod, Janene Caywood, Jason Lyons, Ritchie Doyle, Jim Parker, and Brian Smith.

The Archeological Resources Protection Act

Archeological resources and historic objects on Federal lands are protected by law. The digging, collecting, or damage of these resources on Federal lands without a permit is a felony offense punishable by fines up to $100,000 or imprisonment or both.

Note from the Publisher

I first encountered Ralph S. Space's *The Lolo Trail* one Christmas holiday at Lochsa Lodge just over Lolo Pass from my hometown of Missoula. We had tons of snow that winter, and the family skied all day, hit the hot springs at twilight, then retired to the warmth of our cabins. I found *The Lolo Trail* at breakfast one morning.

And here it is, more than a decade later, and I'm delighted at the opportunity to publish this second edition.

If you're unfamiliar with the terrain, Route 12, the Lolo Highway, is not the Lolo Trail. In fact, for most of its run from the heights of Lolo Pass in Montana through to Weippe, Idaho, the Lolo Trail is a long way from the highway. The Trail follows the ridgetops between five thousand and seven thousand feet.

You mustn't attempt to explore this rugged landscape without thoughtful preparation and adequate equipment. Please check the weather reports before you attempt this crossing. As the author, Ralph Space suggests, it can snow all twelve months of the year.

If you're not used to the vagaries of traveling deep in the Rocky Mountains, you may want to hire an outfitter to guide your passage. The best way to experience this journey is to backpack or ride horses or mountain bikes, and an outfitter will make this an enjoyable experience, particularly if your children are along.

The Trail is a National Historic Landmark and is very fragile. In fact, the Lolo and Clearwater National Forests are planning to limit travel during the Lewis and Clark Bicentennial, 2003 to 2006. You must plan ahead and apply for a permit before you set out. On page 131, you will find a listing of licensed outfitters and information about the permit system.

Enjoy.

Jeffrey J. Smith
April 2001

This road is winding, crooked, and rough,
But you can make it, if you are tough.
God help your tires, God help your load,
God bless the men who built this road.

*A jingle Ralph S. Space wrote to describe
the Lolo Trail to those who had never seen it*

A Welcome by Josiah Blackeagle Pinkham

Welcome to Nez Perce Country. Please enjoy your stay while visiting our homeland. The Lolo Trail is filled with national treasures that are interesting to the rest of the public as well as being sacred to the people of the Nez Perce Tribe. Please refrain from removing any part of the trailway. Not only is this disrespectful, it is also a felony punishable by fines and/or imprisonment.

Tribal members also use the different sites along the Trail for many different purposes and this is a right retained by the Nez Perce people through treaties and must be respected. There will be Nez Perce tribal members using the Lolo Trailway for ceremonial activities, and one should always be mindful that these activities are sacred. When you see tribal members involved in any traditional activities, wait until they are completed with what they are doing before you approach them. Out of respect, we caution visitors not to stare at people when they encounter tribal members involved in ceremonial activities such as root digging, hunting, and fishing.

For those of you who are recreationists (hikers, campers, hot spring enthusiasts, etc.), please remember that the Trail is also the place for traditional cultural activities. Please enjoy your visit and be careful.

Josiah Pinkham

Josiah Blackeagle Pinkham
Ethnographer
Nez Perce Tribe

Preface by Stephen E. Ambrose

It was Ralph Space who first got me and my family and some twenty of my students on a week-long hike in Lewis and Clark's footsteps on the Lolo Trail. It was 1976. I wasn't sure our children were up to it. I wondered about my students from New Orleans up in the Idaho mountains. Then I read *The Lolo Trail* and I was determined to do it. We went to Lolo Pass to meet the author. He was delighted we were following the Lewis and Clark Expedition and most of all we were backpacking across the Bitterroot Mountains. He was full of advice on good places to camp and sites to see.

We made the trip, a copy of Space's book in our hands. It was a glorious experience. The scenery, of course, but also immersing ourselves in the history of the Lolo Trail, thanks to the book, and sitting around a campfire on a spot where the Expedition camped, reading aloud from their Journals, made it entrancing. We never got lost and we saw the sites associated with the Trail—in both cases thanks to Space's book.

When we finished we met with Space for a debriefing. How much snow at Indian Post Office two days ago, he wanted to know. What is it like here, there, all over? Any bears? Deer? Birds? And more. Then he asked us about where we had been and where we were going. He was especially interested in our five children, the oldest Stephanie (age sixteen years). How did they like camping for a summer? Were they good hikers? Were they good historians? Were they inspired by the stories they were hearing? He liked their answers.

Just as anyone likes *The Lolo Trail*. It is an excellent travel guide and a fine piece of history. And Space is a good writer who knows how to tell a story.

Stephen E Ambrose

Introduction by Bud Moore

Kansas-born Ralph Space moved, at age one, with the family to Idaho in 1902 and grew up on a ranch located between Weippe and Pierce. At eighteen, he began work for the U.S. Forest Service and hiked the Lolo Trail for the first time in 1924. Following several assignments in other parts of the Northern Rockies, he returned to his home country as supervisor of the Clearwater National Forest. His homecoming allowed him to renew his avocation: finding and recording the Clearwater's history, including that of the Lolo Trail.

On occasion, daughter Judy accompanied Ralph as he searched for tread and artifacts along the Lolo Trail. While he worked, she took photos. Judy says, "He thought it important that those things be found and preserved before they were lost. Dad took time. Never missed a thing in the woods."

Ralph retired from government service in 1963 but continued to devote vigorous attention to history. In 1970 he published *The Lolo Trail*, highly respected for its accuracy by recreationists and professional historians alike. He died in June 1993 at age 92.

Thanks, Ralph and Judy, from all of us who have known the Lolo Trail.

No one knows who or when the first people began to wear the tread leading across the Bitterroot Mountains from Lolo, Montana, to Weippe, Idaho, long known as the Lolo Trail. I first saw the Trail in the 1920s where its worn path wound its way through our favored hunting country in the Lolo Creek tributary of Montana's Bitterroot River. From Woodman Creek to near Lolo Hot Springs, the Trail avoided dense riparian vegetation, narrows, and springtime flood waters by passing through steep but more open terrain north of the valley. That's why Lolo Creek's homesteaders and we meat hunters called it the "High Water Trail."

We knew then that the old Trail was once the Road to the Buffalo for the Nimepoo (Nez Perce) people and the Road to the Salmon for the Salish. We also knew that the Nez Perce made their last journey as a free nation over this Trail pursued by General Howard. And we were reminded in our local elementary school that the Lewis and Clark Expedition had crossed the mountains via the Lolo Trail in 1805 and returned in 1806, a significant event in the Euro-American occupation of the Indian's West.

By the 1920s the once-busy Trail was little used and fading, yet for us it remained a dependable reference. Family talks often included statements like, "Dad shot that buck just above where the Trail crosses Camp Creek." It was the only continuous trail that passed through our realm, coming from and leading to faintly understood somewheres, always beckoning us to explore beyond our local environs. With the day's hunt finished, we would oftimes walk the Trail homeward as darkness fell over the mountains. Our boots would fall softly on the old Trail's tread. We spoke little, our voices subdued by the silence of the land. Emerging expectations of formative youth joined footsteps reaching back in ancient times far beyond our own culture and even the connected memories of generations of Nimepoo and Salish. At times like that the people of the past, their Trail, and the pristine land was beginning to whisper where we have been, who we are, and what we might become. The High Water (Lolo) Trail, then, was an important part of the Spirit of the place where we lived.

I would learn in time that as the Trail was for us in the Lolo Creek Valley, so it was for many others all across the mountains.

Time, forest fires, weather, and activities of humankind have changed the landscape a great deal since the Lewis and Clark Expedition crossed and recrossed those mountains. The Great Western Migration bypassed the Bitterroots yet the Trail remained for years an important foot travel and pack train shortcut from Montana to the water transportation leading to the Pacific Ocean. Much of the Trail in both the east and west outskirts of the mountains disappeared as early-day homesteaders tilled arable land. When commercial logging pushed deeper into the mountains, more of the Trail and its associated artifacts were degraded or lost. With the buffalo gone from the eastern prairies and the Indians resettled to small reservations, the need for the Trail diminished. And, for a time, so did the recognition of the Trail's historical and cultural value.

The Trail's character and use also shifted when in 1934 the U.S. Forest Service completed construction of the first motorway (truck trail) across the mountains in the Lochsa-Selway region to provide motorized access for fire protection. The motorway followed near the Trail, obliterating some sections but leaving various stretches in near original condition. After 1934 we could, during short, high-mountain summers, cross the mountains by automobile. The horsemen of the Nez Perce's Road to the Buffalo were yielding to the drivers of cars and trucks. Although the Lewis and Clark Highway (Route 12) did not follow close to the Trail, its completion in 1962 provided the access long sought by the people of Idaho and Montana. Since then the Lolo Trail and its motorway have been used primarily by the Forest Service, hunters, outfitters, recreationists, and individuals and organizations interested in rediscovering, protecting, and promoting the history of the Trail.

Creation, in 1965, of the Nez Perce National Historic Park brought nationwide attention to the Trail. Magazine articles and books now tout the Trail's historic, spiritual and cultural values, and natural attractions. The Lewis and Clark Bicentennial is expected to draw many tourists to the area. In that frame of reference, the Lolo Trail, once the great road to the buffalo, for a time obscured by the Manifest Destiny of western occupation, has arisen from near obscurity to a national, spiritual, historic, economic, and cultural treasure for us all.

Beginning on either end, after crossing an array of private land acquired through settlement and land grant procedures, the land hosting the Lolo Trail is primarily National Forest, state, and large industrial ownerships. And the managers of these lands recognize the Trail's significance. For example, Lewis and Clark's Thirteen-Mile and Glade Creek campsites were located on Plum Creek Timber Company lands, and the company's policy has long been to protect the Trail's tread and associated artifacts. They subsequently sold the Glade Creek site to the State of Idaho. The Lolo National Forest recently acquired land or easements from Plum Creek to bring most of the Trail from Graves Creek to Lolo Pass into public ownership. The State of Montana has acquired fifteen acres of Lewis and Clark's Travellers Rest campsite near Lolo, Montana. And on the west end, from the Clearwater Forest boundary to Weippe, Idaho, the Trail with a few exceptions crosses industrialized and state forest ownership where managers protect the Trail's tread by modifying timber harvest and grazing practices.

The stewards of the Clearwater National Forest have designated a one-half-mile wide Lolo Trail Corridor, which encompasses the Lolo Trail, Nee-me-poo Trail, Nez Perce National Historic Trail, Bird-Traux Wagon Road, and the Lolo Motorway. Designated sites within Nez Perce National Historic Park are also included. For the past several years Forest Service personnel, interested individuals, historic organizations, and members of the Nez Perce Nation have been developing an inventory of historical and ancient resources within the corridor. When finished, the inventory will furnish detailed information needed by federal, state, and private land managers to join with the interested citizenry and prepare a plan for protection, stewardship, and sustainable use of the corridor's resources.

The Lolo Trail is a place where we can recapture the Spirit of ancient and historic peoples. Its several treads wind across a variety of once-natural ecosystems. And each of us can go there and see, for better or worse, the effects on the land of more recent occupation and human use. We can learn from that and apply those lessons in future stewardship. As it has always been for the Nimepoo, the Spirit of the Trail, wherever we can find it, remains strong and available for all of us. Yet, like the ecosystems that surround it, the Trail and its environs are fragile, subject to degradation by overuse, commercial exploitation, too much access, and heavy footsteps.

There's life in the Lolo Trail. So, let's hang on to that life, hold close to nature and walk softly as we rediscover and protect its Spirit. That way, what remains of the Trail can always whisper where we have been, who we are, and what we might become.

Bud Moore

THE LOLO TRAIL

Chapter 1

KUSEYNE 'ISKIT

The Old Indian Trail

The Lolo Trail, strictly speaking, is the travel route from Lolo, Montana, to Weippe, Idaho. The route has had a number of names and its terminus has changed from time to time. This book will have as its main topic events concerned with this trail, but I will go beyond its geography when that is necessary to complete a story or bring it to a logical ending.

The Indians traveled the Lolo Trail before the coming of white men. The Nez Perce name for this route is *Kuseyne 'Iskit*[1] or buffalo trail. It was one of several routes of travel for the Nez Perce to the buffalo herds in Montana and Wyoming. Another route was farther south and became known as the Southern Nez Perce trail.

Some writers state that this trail is thousands of years old. However, the studies I have made indicate that while part of it is very old, a large part of it has been used only a few hundred years, probably after the Indians of this locality acquired horses, or about 1700 A.D.

My studies have consisted of collecting artifacts along the Lolo Trail, Lochsa, and North Fork Rivers[2] and comparing them with those collected elsewhere and classified by age. My study is not conclusive and later findings may prove me wrong, but it appears that before the coming of the horse, the Indians used the rivers as their principal travel routes. This made it necessary to travel cross-country by foot from the head of navigation on one river to the next[3, 4].

Indications are that the Lolo Trail from Lolo, Montana, to

3

The ancient trail can still be found along the north side of Lolo Canyon in Montana.

Wendover Creek is very old. Lewis and Clark found the trail running to the river much deeper than the one over the mountains. This part of the Lolo Trail was used by the Salish Indians in reaching the salmon fishing areas around Powell Ranger Station, there being no salmon in the waters of the Clark Fork River. From artifacts found, I believe this part of the Lolo Trail older than the remainder. Another feature of the Lolo Trail that supports my theory is that, at the time of Lewis and Clark, the trail ran from meadow to meadow. Apparently this was done to insure horse feed, when a much shorter route with fewer changes in grade could have been developed.

The Lolo Trail was a formidable obstacle to the early explorers, trappers, hunters, and soldiers. It is often described as precipitous, boulder-strewn, and over high, rugged mountains. It is none of these. The highest point on the trail is 7035 feet at Indian Post Office, which is not high as mountains go. Boulders are rare and there isn't a single cliff to be seen in the entire route.

What, then, made this trail so difficult to cross? There are a number of things.

First, the area is heavily timbered. Each year dead trees rot off and fall, others are blown over by the wind or broken off by snow. Even one year's crop of downed trees would make travel difficult, and the accumulation of several years make travel slow and dangerous to horses.

Second, snow comes early and melts late. Snow may fall any month, but winter snow can come as early as October 1 and leaves sometime between July 1 and 20.

Third, there is little game along the Lolo Trail. Game animals do cross this divide but prefer the basins at the heads of streams for their feeding grounds[5].

Fourth, the ridge this trail follows is not a hogback but a series of mountains and deep saddles. The divide is cut by six major saddles and many more small ones so that the traveler is continually dropping into deep saddles and then climbing out the other side. For example, the elevation as Sherman Saddle is about forty-eight hundred feet and Sherman Peak sixty-five hundred feet, a climb of about seventeen hundred feet in three miles.

General Howard's description of the Lolo Trail illustrates this point[6]. "It does not appear far to the next peak. It is not so in a straight course, but such a course is impossible. 'Keep to the hogback.' That means that there usually is a crooked connecting ridge between two neighboring heights and you must keep on it. The necessity of doing so often made the distance three times greater than by straight lines; but the ground was too stony, too steep, the canyon too deep, to attempt the shorter course. Conceive this climbing ridge after ridge, in the wildest of wilderness, with the only possible pathway filled with timber, small and large, crossed and crisscrossed; and now, while the horses and mules are feeding on innutritious wire grass, you will not wonder at only sixteen miles a day."

Fifth, the Clearwater mud. The Clearwater country is blessed with a deep fertile soil that becomes slick and deep mud when wet.

5

Chapter 2

LOLO
How the Name Originated

In David Thompson's journals[7] he states that he met Michael, Lolo, and Gregoire on March 18, 1810, on Camas Creek near the present town of Perma, Montana. The same party visited him at his Salish House, near Thompson Falls, on April 1 and traded a few skins. Then on April 11, 1810, David Thompson states that Lolo killed a doe.

Apparently this man was a free trapper, that is, he was not attached to any fur company. Likely he was of French descent since the men with whom he traveled bore French names.

Judge Woody, an early citizen of Missoula, Montana, states that Lolo Creek in Montana was named for a trapper who had a cabin on Graves Creek, a branch of Lolo Creek, and was buried there. He did not give any other name for him. Jack Harlan, a historian of Clearwater County, says his complete name was Lawrence Rence. There being no "r" in either the Flathead or Nez Perce languages, Lawrence was pronounced Lou-Lou, Lo Loo, or Lo Lo because they could not say Lawrence. It appears in all three forms in early writings.

I am unable to confirm the name Lawrence Rence. It does not appear in the early writings. However, I am able to confirm that a trapper by the name of Lou-Lou or Lolo was buried on Graves Creek.

The late Harry Wheeler[8], a well-educated Nez Perce much interested in local history, told me that Lolo had a Nez Perce wife and lived on Graves Creek.

Graves Creek, which flows into Lolo Creek, is where the trapper, Lou-Lou or Lolo, lived.

Wheeler also told a story about Lolo and a Kootenai Indian companion who came upon a grizzly bear at close quarters. Lolo shot the bear but only wounded it. The bear charged. The Indian succeeded in getting up a tree, but the bear trapped Lolo under a windfall and dragged him out, almost tearing his leg off. The Kootenai, who was armed with a bow, shot arrows into the bear until it left the area. Lolo was taken to his cabin, but he died and was buried beneath a beautiful grove of pine trees near the meadow. Wheeler, although able to describe the area quite accurately, had never been there.

I was taken to this grave in 1939 by W. W. White, an early employee of the Forest Service and one time Supervisor of the Lolo National Forest. At that time the area had not been logged, and Wheeler's description fit perfectly. There was a mound marked with a headstone.

I tried to find this grave again in 1963 but the area had been logged and leveled with a bulldozer. I then tried a mine detector, hoping that Lolo's rifle had been buried with him as was the custom of the Nez Perce Indians, but I had no success. I inquired about the grave among some of the old residents of the area. All they could tell me was that there used to be a grave there, but they could no longer locate it.

The earliest reference to the name applied to the Montana Lolo Creek—as opposed to Lolo Creek in Idaho—is by John Work, who called it the Lo Loo or Lou Lou. His writing is not clear[9].

There are those who believe that the name Lolo originated through corruption of the French name Le Louis given to the trail in honor of Meriwether Lewis. If this were true, it seems that the spelling would have been Le Lou or La Lou.

In 1866 Wellington Bird and Major Truax widened and relocated part of the Lolo Trail. Major E. A. Fenn, Supervisor of the Clearwater National Forest—from 1902 to 1903 and from 1907 to 1910—stated that he had heard reports that Major Truax named the trail in honor of Lola Montez, a beautiful Irish dancer and adventuress, whose real name was Gilbert[10]. Since an early map of the area prepared by DeLacy shows both the Idaho and Montana Lolo Creeks named prior to 1865 and the name given by Truax would have been Lola, this source may

8

well be doubted.

A fourth possibility for the name Lolo is that the Chinook word for pack is Lolo. However, this appears to be a coincidence.

Captain Pierce referred to the Lolo Trail as the trail to the Lo Lo Fork. Apparently the miners around Pierce and old Oro Fino used that name and in all probability that is why the name Lolo was applied to the Idaho stream, which the Indians called Nawah. The first "a" is long.

Even as late as 1895 Carlin referred to the Creek in Montana as the Lou-Lou, the stream in Idaho as Lolo, the trail as Lo Lo$_{11}$, and the town in Montana as Lo Lo.

Finally, the name for every person and every place settled down to Lolo. After considering all possibilities, I strongly favor the belief that the name Lolo came from the fur trapper.

Chapter 3

LEWIS AND CLARK
The expedition's western crossing in 1805

The Lewis and Clark Expedition crossed the Lolo Trail going west in 1805 and returned in 1806. So far as can be proved they were the first white people to cross the trail although an Indian legend says that another party preceded them. However, this appears doubtful, since at the time of Lewis and Clark, no mention is made of this. The Indians did say they had seen white men on the Lower Columbia.

Lewis and Clark had been warned by Toby, their Shoshoni guide, that the trail was difficult, but it was far worse than they expected. On its way west the party went through its most difficult trials. The thirty-two men—with Sacajewea and her baby Pomp—ran into a snowstorm and almost froze. They killed little game, finally managing to arrive, hungry and exhausted, at the friendly Indian camp at Weippe.

On their way back, they dreaded this formidable obstacle and worried about it long before they reached it. They spent valuable days at Kamiah waiting for the snows to melt, and their first attempt was unsuccessful. Then, because of the generosity of the Nez Perce Indians who furnished them with fine horses and three expert guides, they made it.

Let us trace their journey day by day, using the diaries kept by various members of the party[12]. These diaries lack punctuation and since there were no dictionaries or standards of spelling at that time, each writer spelled in accordance with his own peculiar method of pronunciation. To make the diaries easier to read, I will use modern spelling and punctuation. I will also follow the quotation of each day's diary with my comments, stating where I believe the events took place. I will also comment on other parts of their diaries that I believe might be interesting to the reader. I will attempt to locate the modern U.S. Forest Service campgrounds and other landmarks so that anyone who so desires may use this chapter to orient himself on the ground.

The Lewis and Clark party was a military expedition sent by Congress at the request of President Jefferson to explore the country from St. Louis, Missouri, via the Missouri River, to the Pacific Ocean. At Lolo, Montana, it was composed of twenty-nine members of the Army, York, the slave, Sacajawea and her baby, and two Shoshone Indian guides, making a party of thirty-four.

September 9, 1805. Lewis:

> We continued our route down the west side of the river [Bitterroot] about five miles further and camped on a large creek [Lolo] which falls in on the left. As our guide informed me that we should leave the river at this place and the weather appearing settled and fair, I determined to halt the next day, rest our horses and take some celestial observations. We call this Traveler's Rest. It is about 20 yards wide with a fine, bold, clear running stream.

Whitehouse, in his diary, states in part:

> Camped on a plain near a creek which runs into the River about 2 miles below.

Comment: The exact spot at which Lewis and Clark camped is unknown. Most historians say at the mouth of Lolo Creek near the present town of Lolo.

In Lewis' diary on the return trip, June 30, 1806, he states: "we arrived at our old encampment on the south side of the creek a little above its entrance into Clarks Fork [Bitterroot]." I have also checked the mileage according to the log of their journey and their camp would have to be up Lolo Creek to make the distances check. I agree with 0. D. Wheeler[13] that the camp was on the south side of Lolo Creek about one mile above the town of Lolo. This camp is not marked, although there is a historical marker on Highway 12 near Lolo.

[Publisher's Note: Almost certainly Traveler's Rest is on land owned for more than thirty years by Pat and Ernie Deschamps on the south side of Lolo Creek more than a mile upstream from the confluence. The coordinates of the latitude and longitude recorded by Lewis and Clark match the Deschamps' place. Survey maps from the 1870s trace the aboriginal trail through the property, and infrared photos taken in July 1996 reveal two rows of teepee rings on the site.]

September 10, Lewis:

> The morning being fair I sent out all the hunters and directed two of them to proceed down the river as far as its junction with the Eastern fork [Clarks Fork] which heads near the Missouri. . . . I think this river continues its course along the Rocky Mts. Northwardly as far or perhaps beyond the sources of the Medicine River and then turning to the west falls into the Tacootchetessee [Fraser River]. . . . This evening one of our hunters returned accompanied by three men of the Flathead Nation whom he had met in his excursion up Traveler's Rest Creek. . . . We learned from these people that two men whom they suppose to be of the Snake Nation had stolen 23 horses from them and they were in pursuit of the thieves. They told us they were in great haste. . . . The sun was now set, two of them departed after receiving a few articles we gave them, and the third remained having agreed to continue with us as a guide, and to introduce us to his relations whom he informed us were numerous and resided in the plains below the mountains on the Columbia River, from whence, he said, the water was good and capable of being navigated to the sea; that some of his relations were at sea last fall and saw an old white man who resided there by himself and who had given them some handkerchiefs such as he saw in our possession. He said it would require five sleeps.

Comment: It is sometimes asked why Lewis and Clark did not go down the Clark Fork River. From Lewis' diary he believed the Clark Fork to be a branch of the Fraser River. Whitehouse says: "Our guides tell us these waters run into the Mackenzie River as near as they can give account, but he is not acquainted that way. So we go the road he

Lolo Peak is the major geographical landmark along the Lolo Trail near the Bitterroot Valley of Montana.

knows." The last sentence summed up the situation.

Although Lewis says in his diary that their three visitors were Flatheads, they were actually Nez Perce. For a time Lewis and Clark called both the Flatheads and the Nez Perce Indians Flatheads. Five days journey from Lolo as the Indians traveled would put the traveler in Nez Perce country.

[Nez Perce ethnographer Josiah Blackeagle Pinkham says that although they are two distinct, sovereign nations, the Nez Perce and Flathead share some cultural attributes. It is also true that the Nez Perce and Flathead have intermarried for many generations.]

It was unfortunate that the party lost their Nez Perce guide for as we will see on the return journey these men knew the trail intimately.

September 11, Clark:

> The loss of two of our horses detained us Until 3 P.M. Our Flathead Indian being restless thought proper to leave us and proceed on alone. Sent out the hunters to hunt in advance as usual. . . . We proceeded on up the Creek [Lolo] on the right side through a narrow valley and good road for 7 miles and

Today, Lolo Creek flows through several large cattle ranches near Woodman Creek.

encamped at some old Indian lodges. Nothing killed this evening. Hills on the right high and rugged. The mountains on the left [Lolo Peak] high and covered with snow.

Comment: Notice that the rains of the past few days were snow at higher elevations. The party will have difficulty with snow later.

The camp of September 11 is marked on Highway 12, although I believe the marker is too far east. I would put this camp about one half mile east of Woodman Creek.

September 12, Clark:

A white frost. Set out at 7 o'clock and proceed up the Creek [Lolo]. Passed a fork on the right [Woodman Creek] on which I saw, near an old Indian encampment, a sweat house covered with earth. At two miles ascended a high hill and proceeded through a hilly and thickly covered country for 9 miles and on the right of the creek, passing several branches from the right of fine clear water, and struck at a fork [Graves Creek] at which place the road forks, one passing up each fork. . . . Continued on and passed on the sides of the steep, stony mountains, which might be avoided by keeping up the creek, which is thickly covered with undergrowth and fallen timber.

14

Lolo Hot Springs draws travelers to its roadside attractions: a campground, restaurant, and motel.

Crossed a mountain 8 miles without water and encamped on a hillside on the Creek after descending a long, steep mountain. Some of our party did not get up until 10 P.M. I made camp at 8 P.M.

On this Creek, and particularly on this road, the Indians have peeled a number of pine for the bark, which they eat at certain seasons. Our hunters killed only one pheasant [ruffed grouse] this afternoon. Party and horses much fatigued.

Comment: The first creek crossed is Woodman Creek. The trail left Lolo Creek bottom at the western end of Woodman Meadows and ascended a low saddle. The fork in the road was at Graves Creek. The right fork went up Graves Creek and down Petty Creek to the Clark Fork River near Alberton, Montana. Old maps show such a trail. The high hill they crossed is Cedar Run Ridge between Howard Creek to the east and Powell Meadows to the west. They camped two miles below Lolo Hot Springs. Gass says they camped on a small branch of Lolo Creek. This camp was where the State of Montana maintenance building now stands. There is a marker on Highway 12 but it is somewhat west of the actual campsite.

[In 2001, the Lolo National Forest purchased more than twelve hundred acres of land from the Plum Creek Timber Company for $1.6 million. This purchase, plus easements on two and a half miles of Plum Creek land near the top of Lolo Pass, consolidates public ownership of the fourteen miles of the Lolo Trail from Graves Creek to Lolo Pass. The National Forest has no plans to modernize the Trail, but instead will keep it primitive to allow visitors to see and experience what Lewis and Clark experienced.]

September 13, Clark:

> A cloudy morning. Captain Lewis and one of our guides lost their horses. Captain Lewis and four men detained to hunt the horses. I proceeded on and at the distance of two miles passed several springs which I observed the deer and elk had made roads to, and below one the Indians had made a hole to bathe. I tasted the water and found it hot and not bad tasting. I found this water nearly boiling hot at the place it spouted from the rocks. I put my finger in the water, at first could not bear it in a second.
>
> As several roads led from these springs in different directions, my guide took a wrong road and took us out of our road 3 miles. After falling on the right road, I proceeded on through a tolerable route for 4 or 5 miles and halted to let our horses graze, as well as to wait for Captain Lewis, who had not yet come up. The Creek is very much dammed up by beaver but we can see none. Dispatched two men back to look for Lewis' horses after he came up, and we proceeded over a mountain to the head of the Creek [Lolo], which we left to our left, and at a place 6 miles from the place I nooned, we fell on a small Creek [Pack] from the left, which passed through open glades, some of which were one half mile wide.
>
> We proceeded down this Creek about two miles to where the mountains close on either side and encamped. I shot four pheasants of the common kind except the tail was black. Shields killed a blacktail deer.

Comment: The hot springs are, of course, what are now known as Lolo Hot Springs, but once called Boyle's Springs. The trail went up Lolo Creek to above Lee Creek. From there it climbed over Wagon Mountain and came down to Packer Meadows.

***The snow comes early and stays late at
Packer Meadows on Lolo Pass.***

[Hot springs have long been considered sacred sites to the Nez
Perce. Individual members of the tribe have used hot springs for thera-
peutic and medicinal purposes as well as to manufacture bows and
other implements from mountain sheep horns.]

The party is now over the Bitterroot divide on the Lochsa side. It
then went down creek to the lower end of the meadows and camped.

The pheasants were Franklin grouse or fool hens. The deer was a mule deer.

September 14, Whitehouse:

> A cloudy morning. We eat the last of our meat . . .

Clark:

> . . . We crossed a high mountain on the right of the creek for six miles to the forks of the Glade Creek, the right hand fork which falls in is about the size of the other. We crossed to the left side of the forks and cross a very high mountain for nine miles to a large fork from the left which appears to head in the snow topped mountains south.
>
> We cross Glade Creek above its mouth at a place where the Flathead Indians have made a weir to catch salmon and have but lately left the place. I could see no fish, and the grass entirely eaten out by the horses, we proceed on two miles and encamped opposite a small island at the mouth of a small branch on the right side of the river, which is at this place 80 yards wide, swift and stony.
>
> Here we were compelled to kill a colt for our men and selves to eat for want of meat, and we named the South Fork Colt Killed Creek, and this we call Koos Koos Ke. Turned our horses on the island.
>
> Rained, snowed, and hailed the greater part of the day. All wet and cold.

Comment: The party left Packer Meadows and went over the ridge between Crooked Fork and Pack Creek to where Brushy Creek joins the Crooked Fork. They crossed Brushy Creek and went over the ridge between Crooked Fork and Cabin Creek to where the Crooked Fork and Whitesand Creek join to make the Lochsa River, which they called the *Koos Koos Ke* River. They crossed to the north bank of the Lochsa and after traveling two miles camped at Powell Ranger Station. The island is now so heavily timbered that it would not furnish feed for even one horse. The Powell Camp is well marked with a Forest Service sign.

The name *Koos Koos Ke* which Lewis and Clark gave to the present Lochsa and Clearwater Rivers was not a name used by the Nez Perce.

18

The word *Koos* in Nez Perce means water and *Kee* is see. So if the word *Koos Koos Ke* was given a literal translation it would be water water see. Obviously, something else was intended.

[Ethnographer Josiah Pinkham asserts that the spelling should be *Kuus x̂ayx̂aayx̂*, and the words mean "water-clear."]

Koos Keich Keich, according to Josephy, means Clearwater in Nez Perce and he believes it may be that this was the original name, which became misunderstood and misspelled to *Koos Koos Ke*. Many of the younger Indians have now accepted *Koos Koos Ke* as meaning Clearwater. Evidently they adapted it from the whites.

Another explanation of the word is contained in a book written by Frank T. Gilbert in 1882. Here is what he has to say: "The word *Koos Koos Ke*, erroneously supposed to be a Nez Perce word meaning Clearwater, was given to it. P. B. Whitman, the interpreter for the Nez Perce agency, accounts for this error in the following way: The Nez Perces probably, in trying to explain to Lewis and Clark that there were two large streams running through their country, the smaller of which was the one they saw, and the larger one, now called the Snake, repeated the words '*Koots Koots Kee*' and pointed to the visible stream, meaning 'this is the smaller' from which the whites inferred that this was the Indian name. *Kaih-Kaih-Koosh* is the Nez Perce word signifying Clear water."

I discussed the meaning of the words *Koos Koos Ke, Koots Koots Ke* and *Koos Keich Keich* with William Parsons, an 81-year-old Nez Perce of Kooskia. He said that *Koos Keich Keich* does mean the Clearwater and was the name the Nez Perce applied to the present Clearwater below Ahsahka.

Koots Koots means little and *Koots Koots Kee*, as Whitman said, means this is the little one [literally little one see].

Mr. Parsons pointed out another possibility. *Koots Koots Koos* means the little water or Little River. *Koos Koots Kee* also means little river in Nez Perce, so the *Koos Koos Kee* of Lewis and Clark could be one of these with a slight misspelling. It is interesting to note that Samuel Parker called the Clearwater the Coos-Coots-Ke.

This island at Powell Ranger Station is where Lewis and Clark camped on on Sept. 14, 1805.

[Ethnographer Josiah Pinkham says the Nez Perce use the word *Kuus x̂ayx̂aayx̂*, and the misunderstandings probably arose when the explorers could not duplicate the correct pronunciation.]

Lewis and Clark called the Little Missouri the *Koos Koos Annima*. See page 21, Volume 5 of Thwaits *Journals*. Parsons says this should have been *Koots Koots Annima*. Apparently Lewis and Clark left out the "t" in Koots there, and it is logical to assume that they did the same in their name for the Lochsa.

This all appears to add up to the conclusion that the Nez Perce did call at least a part of the Clearwater River by that name, but the word Lewis and Clark applied to it meant the Little River.

The *Lochsa* is a Flathead word meaning rough water.

Packer Meadows was named for a man who built a cabin there, planning to homestead the meadow, but dropped the plan when the land survey gave the Northern Pacific Railway Company land grant rights to a large part of the meadow.

September 15, Clark:

> We set out early, the morning cloudy, and proceeded on down the right side of the River, over steep points, rocky and brushy as usual, for four miles to an old Indian fishing place. Here the road leaves the river to the left and ascends a mountain, winding in every direction to get up the steep ascents and to pass the immense quantity of fallen timber which had fallen from different causes, that is, fire and wind, and has deprived the greater part of the south sides of this mountain of its timber. Four miles up the mountain I found a spring and halted for the rear to come up and let our horses rest and feed. In about two hours the rear of the party came up, much fatigued, and horses more so. Several horses slipped and rolled down steep hills, which hurt them very much. The one which carried my desk and small trunk turned over and rolled down a mountain for 40 yards and lodged against a tree, broke the desk.
>
> The horse escaped and appeared but little hurt. From this point I observed a range of high mountains covered with snow from SE to SW, with their tops bald or void of timber. After two hours delay, we proceeded on up the mountain. When we arrived at the top, we conceived we would find no water and concluded to camp and make use of snow we found on top to cook

The Salish Indians had set up salmon fishing weirs near in mouth of Wendover Creek.

At Whitehouse Pond, the Corps of Discovery left the Lochsa River and climbed to the Lolo Trail.

There are many vistas on the Lolo Trail looking into the Selway-Bitterroot Wilderness to the south.

the remains of our colt and make our soup. Two of our horses gave out, poor and too much hurt to proceed, and left in the rear. Nothing killed today except two pheasants [Ruffed grouse].

Comment: The party went down the north bank of the Lochsa to the ridge between Wendover and Cold Storage Creeks. The fishing place was just below the mouth of Wendover Creek. I have found Indian artifacts there, proving this was an old Indian campground. [Publisher's note: Collection of Indian artifacts on federal property is a felony punishable by fines and/or imprisonment.]

Whitehouse mentions passing a small pond. This pond is now called Whitehouse Pond, as is the Forest Service campground across Highway 12. [The author, Ralph Space, suggested this name for the pond.]

Wendover Creek is named for a trapper who operated in that area.

The party went up Wendover Ridge, which now has a beautiful stand of mature timber and camped on top of an unnamed mountain. The Forest Service has a sign marking the place the old trail crosses Route 12, the present Lolo Highway. [Wayne Fairchild, a local outfitter, warns that this trail is a grueling seven or eight miles climb to "Snow Bank Camp" at the top of the ridge. It takes four to six hours, and it is not well maintained after you leave the trailhead.]

The high snowy mountains were the Bitterroot Mountains south of Lolo Pass.

September 16, Clark:

Began to snow about three hours before day and continued all day. The snow in the morning four inches deep on the old snow, and by night we find it six to eight inches deep. I walked in front to keep the road and found great difficulty in keeping it, as in many places the snow had entirely filled the track and obliged me to hunt several minutes for it. At 12 o'clock we halted on top of the mountain to warm and dry ourselves a little, as well as to let our horses rest and graze a little on some long grass which I observed. The knobs, steep hillsides, and fallen timber continue today, and a thickly timbered country of eight different kinds of pine, which are so covered with snow that in passing through them we are continually covered with snow. I have been wet and as cold in every part as I ever was in my life; indeed, I was at one time fearful my feet would freeze in the

The Lolo Trail passes the Indian Post Office, where rock cairns grace a spectacular overlook.

The "Sinque Hole" rests along a two-mile portion of the Lolo Trail left for hikers and those riding horses.

thin moccasins I wore. After a short delay in the middle of the day, I took one man and proceeded as fast as I could about six miles to a small branch crossing to the right, halted and built fires for the party which arrived at dusk, very cold and much fatigued. We camped at this branch in a thickly timbered bottom, which was scarcely large enough for us to lie level. Men all cold and hungry. Killed a second colt, which we all supped heartily on and thought it fine meat.

I saw four deer today before we set out, which came up the mountain, and what is singular, snapped seven times at a large buck. My gun has a steel fuzee and never snapped seven times before. In examining it, found the flint loose.

Whitehouse says:

. . . We descended the mountain down to a lonesome cave on a creek, where we camped in a thicket of spruce, pine and balsam fir timber.

Whitehouse also says:

Cap. Clark shot at a deer but missed it.

Comment: Hunting stories are often known to disagree but in either case it was a keen disappointment to the hungry party.

The place Lewis and Clark camped on September 16 has been much disputed. It is my belief that they ate lunch at Spring Hill. The distance checks and there is an abundance of grass there.

The Lonesome Cove Camp is almost due north of the Indian Post Office rock cairns. The old trail, parts of which can still be found by careful searching, turned back or switch-backed at the rock cairns and dropped off on the north side and came close to a small timbered flat with a small creek. This is where I believe they camped. The Forest Service has marked this place with a metal stake. [An outfitter, Wayne Fairchild, says that today it's about a mile along the trail from Indian Post Office down to Lonesome Cove Camp.]

The Indian Post Office consists of two rock cairns. They get their name from an old story that the Indians conveyed messages by piling these stones in various ways. However, the Indians state that they had no method of conveying messages by stones except such as directional signs, how many were in a party, or other simple messages. However, the rock piles are very old and were likely there when Lewis and Clark went by, but they do not mention them.

Diaries of the return trip in 1806 make it clear that the trail did leave the divide for several miles and it is likely that this is the place. There is a lake plainly visible from the top of the ridge a short distance west of these cairns, which was not mentioned either in the west or east log, which is further evidence that this is the turn-off point. This may be one of the points where Captain Clark had difficulty in finding the trail.

[Publisher's Note: The U.S. Forest Service commissioneed an intensive archaeological survey of the Lolo Trail by a Missoula firm, Historical Research Associates, in the summer of 2000. Archaeologists concluded that the trail is actually a system of trails. It is no surprise, therefore, that Captain Clark had difficulty finding the trail. Archaeologists believe this corridor contained ever-changing trails that would evolve depending on changes in the landscape brought by fire, forest growth, blow-downs, or other impediments.]

The eight species of the Pine family Clark observed were likely Alpine fir, Grand Fir, Englemann Spruce, Mountain Hemlock, Douglas Fir, Lodgepole Pine, Western White Pine, and White Barked Pine.

September 17, Whitehouse:

> Cold and cloudy. We went out to hunt our horses, but found them much scattered. The mare which owned the colt which we killed went back and led four more horses back to where we took dinner yesterday. Most of the other horses found scattered on the mountain, but we did not find all until noon, at which time we set out and proceeded on. The snow lay heavy on the timber. Passed along a rough road up and down the mountains. Descended down a steep part of the mountain. The afternoon clear and warm. The snow melted so that the water stood in the trail over our moccasins in some places. Very slippery, and bad traveling for our horses. We ascend very high and rocky mountains; some bald places on the top of the mountains, high rocks standing up and high precipices. Crossed several creeks or spring runs in the course of the day. Camped at a small branch on the mountain near a round sinque hole full of water. We, being hungry, obliged us to kill the other suckling colt to eat.

One of the hunters chased a bear, but killed nothing. We expect that there is game near; we hear wolves howl and saw some deer sign.

Clark states:

. . . we camped at a run passing to the left.

Comment: The trail Lewis and Clark followed did not stay on the main divide but dropped down into Moon Creek, crossed Howard Creek, and down to the forks of Gravey and Serpent Creeks, thence up the ridge between these creeks to the main divide. The eastern trip diaries are more descriptive of this route.

The sink hole camp is in the first saddle east of Indian Grave Mountain. There is a small pond here with a creek draining out of it that fits the description perfectly.

The party killed the last of the colts at this camp, and apparently Lewis and Clark got together on a plan of action that night, to decide what should be done about the emergency situation.

September 18, Clark:

A fair, cold morning. I proceeded on in advance with six hunters to try and find deer or something to kill and send back to the party. The want of provisions, together with the difficulty of passing the mountains, dampened the spirits of the party, which induced us to resort to some plan of reviving their spirits. I determined to take a party of the hunters and proceed on in advance to some level country where there was some game, kill some meat, and send it back.

We passed over a country similar to the one of yesterday. More fallen timber. Passed several runs and springs passing to the right. From the top of a high mountain [Sherman Peak] at twenty miles, I had a view of an immense plain and level country to the SW and W. At a great distance a high mountain beyond the plain. Saw but little sign of deer and nothing else. Made 32 miles and encamped on a bold running creek passing to the left, which I call Hungry Creek, as at that place we had nothing to eat. I halted only one hour to let our horses feed on a grassy hillside and rest. Drewyer shot at a deer but didn't get it.

Comment: Clark is now in the lead with six men.

The U.S. Forest Service tries to restrict vehicle travel on the side roads in spite of occasional vandalism.

The high mountain from which Clark saw the extensive plain is Sherman Peak. The plain they saw was the open grass country extending northwest from Grangeville and is today called the Camas and Nez Perce Prairies. The high mountain beyond was likely Cottonwood Butte, but it may have been the Blue Ridge Mountains in Oregon, which also can be seen from Sherman Peak.

Hungry Creek became known as Obia Creek, and so appears on old maps. At my suggestion, its name has been changed back to Hungry Creek. Obia is now a branch of Hungry Creek. Clark camped just above where Doubt Creek enters Hungry Creek.

September 18, Lewis [Whitehouse and Gass were with Lewis]:

> Clark set out this morning to go ahead with six hunters. There being no game in these mountains we concluded it would be better for one of us to take the hunters and provide some provisions, while the others remained with and brought up the party. The latter was my part.
>
> Accordingly, I directed the horses be gotten up early, being determined to force my march as much as the abilities of the horses would permit. The negligence of one of the party

[Willard], who had a spare horse, in not attending to him and bringing him up last evening, was the cause of our detention this morning until 8:30 A.M., when we set out. I sent Willard back to search for his horse and proceeded on with the party. At 4 P.M. he overtook us without the horse.

We marched 18 miles this day and camped on the side of a steep mountain. We suffered for water today, passing one rivulet only. We were fortunate in finding water in a deep ravine about one-half mile from camp.

This morning we finished the last of our colt. We supped on a scant portion of portable soup, a few canisters of which, a little bear oil, and about 20 pounds of candles, form our stock of provisions, our only resources being our guns and horses. The first is but a poor dependence where there is nothing upon earth but ourselves, a few pheasants, small grey squirrels, and a blue bird of the vulture kind about the size of a turtle dove or jay bird. Used snow for cooking.

Comment: The water the party crossed was at Indian Grave. The old trail went above the water at Bald Mountain. The blue bird was a Steller's Jay. Lewis' camp of September 18 is about three miles west of Bald Mountain and is marked by a Forest Service sign.

September 19, Clark:

Set out early. Proceeded up Hungry Creek, passing through a small glade at six miles, at which place we found a horse. I directed him killed and hung up for the party after taking breakfast off for ourselves, which we thought fine.

After breakfast proceed on up the creek two miles and left it to our right. Passed over a mountain and the head of a branch of Hungry Creek [Fish Creek], two high mountains, ridges and through much fallen timber which caused our road of today to be double the direct distance of our course. Struck a large creek passing to our left which I kept down for 4 miles and left to our left and passed over a mountain, bad fallen timber, to a small creek passing to our left and encamped. I killed two pheasants [Ruffed grouse] but few birds to be seen. As we descend the mountain the heat becomes more perceptible every mile.

Comment: The glade where the horse was killed is on Hungry Creek about one quarter of a mile from Windy Saddle. The party crossed to the head of Fish Creek then over the divide and down a ridge to

Eldorado Creek, down Eldorado Creek two miles, over a ridge to Cedar Creek and camped.

The campground on Cedar Creek is marked by a Forest Service sign. There is also a splendid grove of large western red cedar there called the Lewis and Clark Grove.

September 19, Lewis:

> Set out this morning a little after sunrise and continued our route about the same course as yesterday for six miles. When the ridge terminated and we, to our inexpressible joy, discovered a large tract of prairie country lying to the SW and widening as it appeared to extend to the west. Through that plain, the Indian [Toby, their Shoshone guide] informed us, the Columbia River of which we are in search runs. This plain appears to be about 60 miles distant, [actually about 40] but our guide assured us we should reach its border by tomorrow. The appearance of this country, our only hope of subsistence, greatly revived the spirits of the party, already reduced and much weakened for want of food.
>
> After leaving the ridge, we ascended and descended several steep mountains, in the distance of six miles further struck a creek [Hungry] about 15 yards wide, our course along this creek upwards, passing two of its branches which flowed in from the north. First at the place we struck the creek [Doubt Creek] and the other three miles further [Bowl Creek].
>
> The road excessively dangerous along this creek, being a narrow, rocky path generally on the side of a precipice. The course upwards due west. We camped on the star side in a little ravine having traveled 18 miles. We took a small amount of portable soup and retired much fatigued. Several men are unwell of dysentery, breaking out or eruptions of the skin.

Comment: The mountain from which Lewis saw the plain was Sherman Peak. The joy of seeing the open country to the SW is best expressed by Gass who wrote:

> When this discovery was made there was as much joy and rejoicing among the corps, as happens among passengers at sea, who have experienced a dangerous protracted voyage, when they first discover land on the long looked for coast.

Whitehouse states that after seeing the plains they:

Sargent Gass called Weippe "a fine, large valley, clear of these dismal and horrible mountains."

... descended three miles, then ascended another mountain as bad as any we have been up before. It made the sweat run off our horses and ourselves."

This is a vivid description of the trip from Sherman Saddle to the top of the mountain to the west.

The party reached Hungry Creek at the mouth of Doubt Creek. The second is Bowl Creek. The little creek on which they camped is unnamed and unmarked except for a metal stake. It rises near Green Saddle. I have suggested that it be named Soup Creek.

September 20, 1805. Clark:

> I set out early and proceeded on through a country as rugged as usual. Passed over a low mountain into the forks of a large creek [Lolo and Eldorado], which I kept down two miles, and ascended a high, steep mountain, leaving the creek to our left hand. Passed the head of several drains on a dividing ridge and at 12 miles descended the mountain to a level pine country. Proceeded on through a beautiful country for three miles to a small plain in which I found many Indian lodges. At the distance of one mile from the lodges I met three Indian boys. When they saw me, they ran and hid themselves in the grass. I dismounted, gave my gun and horse to one of the men, searched and found two of the boys, gave them small pieces of ribbon and sent them forward to the village. Soon after a man came out to meet me, with great caution, and conducted me to a large, spacious lodge, which he told me by signs was the lodge of his great chief, who had set out three days previous with all the warriors of the nation to war on a southwest direction, and would return in 15 or 18 days. The few men who were left in the village, and great numbers of women, gathered around me with much apparent signs of fear, and appeared pleased. They gave us a small piece of buffalo meat, some dried salmon, berries and roots in different states, some round and some like an onion, which they call *pas-she-co*. Of this they make bread and soup. They also gave us the bread made of this root, all of which we ate heartily. I gave them a few small articles as presents, and proceeded on with a chief to his village 2 miles in the same plain, where we were treated kindly in their way, and continued with them all night.
>
> These two villages consist of about 30 double lodges, but few men, a number of women and children. They call them-

selves Chopunnish or pierced noses. Their dialect appears very different from the Flatheads although originally the same people. They are darker than the Flatheads. I have seen dress similar, with more white and blue beads, brass and copper in different forms, shells, and wear their hair in the same way. They are large, portly men, small women, and handsome featured.

Immense quantity of the quamash [camas] or passheco root gathered and in piles about the plain. The roots much like an onion in marshy places. The seeds are in triangular shells on the stalk. They sweat them in the following manner, i.e. dig a hole three feet deep, cover the bottom with split wood, on top of which they lay small stones of about 3 or 4 inches thick, a second layer of split wood, and set the whole on fire, which heats the stones. After the fire is extinguished, they lay grass and mud mixed on the stones, on that dry grass which supports the passheco root a thin coat of grass is laid on top. A small fire is kept, when necessary, in the center of the kiln.

I find myself very unwell all of the evening from eating the fish and roots. Sent out hunters. They kill nothing, but saw some signs of deer.

Comment: Clark left Cedar Creek at Lewis and Clark Grove and climbed the low ridge between Cedar and Lolo Creeks. [Publisher's Note: This is the *Idaho* Lolo Creek.] He then went down this ridge to the forks of Lolo and Eldorado Creeks, crossed Lolo Creek and down it about one mile. From this point he climbed to Crane Meadows which is not shown on most maps. From there he went over the south shoulder of Browns Ridge and down Miles Creek to Weippe Prairie.

He came upon three boys near the Eric Larson ranch. The first village was near the Opresiks' buildings. The second camp was on an arm of the meadow southwest of Weippe. The first road to Weippe came to this arm of the meadow, as did the trail from Weippe to Orofino. There are no markers at either of these campsites.

The name *Weippe* is of Nez Perce Indian origin and is so old it has lost its meaning. Even in 1891 when my father asked some of the old Indians what it meant, they had no answer except that it was the name of a place. The English pronunciation is We-ipe (long i) but the Nez Perce pronounced it oy-yipe. It is a meadow where the Indians gathered camas, raced horses and played games.

Lewis and Clark called the Nez Perce cho-pun-nish, which they said meant pierced noses. Kate McBeth, in her book *The Nez Perces Since Lewis and Clark* says "Lewis and Clark called these Indians the 'Cho-po-nish.'" This was not correct, the word being *Chup-nit-pa-lu,* or people of the pierced noses. Parsons says the correct spelling is Chop-nit-pa-lu, the O is long.

[Ethnographer Josiah Pinkham states that the two most common names the Nez Perce use to describe themselves are *Cuupnitpeh,* meaning "people emerging from the mountains," and *Nimíipuu,* "the people."]

The Nez Perces actually called themselves *ain-e-poo, nim-e-poo,* or *nee-mepoo,* the pronunciation depending on locality, age of the person speaking, and the spelling of the person writing it down. *Nee-me-poo* is now almost universally used by the Nez Perces. What does it mean? Here is what Alice Fletcher, who spent four years with the Nez Perce Indians, while allotting their land has to say: "Their native name 'Nim-e-poo' signified 'the men' or 'the real people,' an appellation commonly used by tribes to distinguish themselves from other peoples." The French called them the Nez Perce (*Ney-per-say*) but this name has been anglicized to Nez Perce or Nezperce. It means pierced noses.

Passheco is a Shoshone word for camas. Later Lewis and Clark called it Quamash. The Nez Perce word is close to *khamas* from which comes the English word camas.

According to Nez Perce legends the Nez Perce considered massacring the party of Clark at Weippe but were persuaded by one of their women named *Wat-ku-ese,* who had been befriended by white people when a captive among Indians to the east, to treat them kindly[14]. Captain Clark knew of no such incident, but he did say that they met an Indian woman who had been as far east as the Mandan village. This statement strongly supports the Indian story.

The Nez Perce, according to McBeth, called the white men *So-yap-po,* the crowned people, because they wore hats. She also says that this is the name *Wat-ku-ese* applied to the white men. Generally speaking the Indians all over America called the white men the long knives. Likely the name she applied to the white men was one that she learned in the east and sounded like *soyappo*, but meant long knives. The Flathead word for long knife is *sooi-api*. To this the Nez Perce would add *poo*, meaning people. The long knives would then be *sooi-api-poo*; a word easily associated with *so-yap-po*. According to Parsons the correct spelling is *so-yahp-poo*.

On September 20, Lewis first describes some birds, which I take to be the flicker, Steller's jay, camp robber or Canadian jay and the three species of grouse common to the Bitterroot Mountains. Then he states:

> We were detained until 10 A.M. in consequence of not being able to collect our horses. We proceeded about two miles when we found the greater part of a horse, which Captain Clark had met with and killed for us. He informed me by note that he would proceed as fast as he could to the level country which lay to the S.W. of us . . . to hunt until our arrival. At one o'clock we halted on a small branch running to the left and made a hearty meal of our horsebeef, much to the comfort of our hungry stomachs. Here I learned that one of the pack horses, with his load, was missing and immediately dispatched Baptist Lapage, who was in charge of him, to search for him. He returned at 3 P.M. without the horse. The load of the horse was of considerable value, consisting of merchandise and all my stock of winter clothing. I, therefore, dispatched two of my best woodsmen to search for him, and proceeded on with the party.
>
> Our route lay through a thick forest of large pine, the general course being S 25 W about 15 miles. We camped on a ridge where there was but little grass for our horses and at a distance from water. However, we obtained as much as served our purpose and supped on our beef.

Comment: Captain Lewis went up Hungry Creek, crossed over into Fish Creek drainage, where he cooked lunch. He then went over the Lochsa Divide and camped on the ridge between Dollar and Sixbit Creeks. This camp is not marked and, so far as I know, it has never been located.

September 21, Clark:

> A fine morning. Sent out all the hunters in different direc-

tions to hunt deer. I, myself, stayed with the Chief to prevent suspicion and to collect by signs as much information as I could about the river and country in advance.

The Chief drew me a kind of chart of the river, and informed me that a greater chief than himself was fishing at the river half a day's march from this village, called Twisted Hair, and that the river forked a little below his camp; and at a long distance below and below two large forks, one from the left [Snake] and the other from the right, [Columbia] the river passed through the mountains [Cascades] at which a great fall of water [The Dalles] passing through the rocks. At these rocks white people lived, from whom they procured the brass, beads, etc., which the women wore.

The chief of another band visited me today and smoked a pipe. I gave a handkerchief and a silver cord, with a little tobacco, to these chiefs.

The hunters all returned without anything. I purchased as much provisions as I could with what things I chanced to have in my pockets, such as salmon, bread, roots and berries and sent R. Fields, with an Indian, to meet Capt. Lewis.

At 4 P.M. set out to the river. Met a man at dark on his way from the river to the village, whom I hired, and gave the neck handkerchief of one of the men, to pilot us to the camp of Twisted Hair. We did not arrive at the camp of Twisted Hair but at a point opposite until 11:30 P.M. Found at this camp 5 squaws and 3 children. My guide called to the Chief, who was camped with two others on an island in the river. He soon joined me and I found him a cheerful man, of about 65, with apparent sincerity. I gave him a medal and smoked until 1 A.M. and went to sleep.

This country from the mountains to the river hills is level, rich, beautiful pine country, badly watered, thinly timbered, and covered with grass. The weather very warm after descending into the low country. The river hills are very high and steep. Small bottoms in the river, which is the Flathead, and is 160 yards wide and shoaley. This is the same river we killed a colt on near a fishing weir. I am very sick today and puke, which relieves me.

Comment: The Indian who mapped the country for Clark showed a remarkable knowledge of the river system to the Dalles. He noted the entrance into the Snake and Columbia Rivers, and even the Cascade Mountains. No doubt he had been to the Dalles. Lewis and Clark later found no white men at the falls, but apparently they had been

The Clearwater River flows through a steep canyon where Clark first saw it.

that far up the Columbia before Lewis and Clark.

Clark traveled from Weippe through the Fraser country and reached the Clearwater River at the mouth of "Village Creek," now Fords Creek. He then came down river to the point where the railroad tunnel is. Twisted Hair was camped on a small island off the point where the Riverside Lumber Company now stands. This is about one mile above Orofino.

[Captain Clark uses the word squaw in his Sept. 21 passage. This word is universally offensive to Indian people and should not be used in modern context.]

Sept. 21, Lewis:

> We were detained this morning until 11 A.M. in consequence of not being able to collect our horses. We set out and proceeded along the ridge on which we encamped, leaving which at one and a half miles we passed a large creek [Eldorado] running to the left just above its junction with another [Dollar] which runs parallel with and on the left of our road before we struck the creek.
>
> Through the level, wide and heavily timbered bottom of this creek [Eldorado] we proceeded for about two and a half miles, when bearing to the right, we passed a broken country heavily timbered, great quantities of which had fallen, and so obstructed our road that it was almost impractical to proceed in many places.
>
> Through these hills we proceeded about 5 miles, when we passed a small creek [Cedar Creek] where Capt. Clark had camped on the 19th. Passing this creek, we continued our route 5 miles through a similar country, when we struck a large creek [Lolo] at its forks.
>
> Passed the north branch [Lolo] and continued down it on the west side one mile and camped in a small open bottom, where there was tolerable feed for our horses. I directed the horses to be hobbled to prevent delay in the morning, being determined to make a forced march tomorrow in order to reach, if possible, the open country.
>
> We killed a few pheasants; I killed a prairie wolf [coyote], which together with our horsebeef and some crawfish which we obtained in the creek, enabled us to make one more hearty meal, not knowing where the next would be found.

Comment: Captain Lewis and party went down the ridge between

A fence outside the post office in Weippe indicates that residents are preparing for the Corps of Discovery's Bicentennial.

Dollar and Six Bit Creeks, crossed Eldorado and went down it two miles. Clark gave a longer distance but Lewis appears correct. Then they crossed over the ridge to Cedar Creek. From there they climbed to the top of the ridge between Cedar and Lolo Creeks. This ridge they followed to the mouth of Eldorado Creek. Here they crossed Lolo Creek and went down it to a small meadow and camped. The camp is marked by a sign which designates it as "Wolf Camp."

On September 22, Clark returned to Weippe with Twisted Hair and his son. In the evening Captain Lewis arrived.

September 22, Gass:

> This was a fine, warm day. About 9 A.M. we continued our march over a ridge, about a west course, upon the top of which is a handsome, small prairie [Crane Meadows]. Here we met one of our hunters with a supply of roots, berries and some fish, which he procured from another band of the Flathead Indians. Captain Clark and the hunters had arrived on the 20th at

41

ful prairie 8 or 9 miles distant from this place. The roots they use are made into a kind of bread which is good and nourishing and like that sometimes made of pumpkins.

We remained here about an hour and then proceed on again down the ridge along a very rough way, and in the evening arrived in a fine, large valley, clear of these dismal and horrible mountains. Here our two men overtook us. They had found the lost horse and clothing, but on their way to us lost both horses.

The Indians belonging to this band received us kindly and appeared pleased to see us and gave us of such provisions as they had. We were at a loss for an interpreter, none of our interpreters being able to understand them. Capt. Clark met us here. He had been over at the river and found the distance about 18 miles and a good road from this place. He thinks we will be able to take the water again.

Comment: Lewis and party left the camp on Lolo Creek and proceeded to Crane Meadows, where they met R. Fields with food. They stopped there to lunch and, no doubt, graze their horses. They then went on to Weippe and camped on a branch of Fords Creek that comes in from the south. The Lewis and Clark party is now united except for the five hunters Clark left at the river.

On September 23, the party stayed at Weippe all day, getting some much needed rest. They ate heartily of the camas, but it did not agree with them, and most of them became ill.

September 24, Clark:

A fine morning. Collected our horses. Dispatched J. Coulter back to hunt the lost horses in the mountains and bring up some shot left behind. At 10 A.M. we set out for the river by the same route I had previously traveled, and at sunset arrived at the island on which I found Twisted Hair. Formed a camp on a large island a little below. Capt. Lewis scarcely able to ride on a gentle horse furnished by the Chief. Several men so unwell they were compelled to lie on the side of the road for some time, others obliged to be put on horses. I give Rush's pills to the sick this evening. Several Indians follow us.

Comment: The party is now camped on what was known as China Island below the tunnel about one mile above Orofino. The railroad fill closed the north channel of the river so this has not been an island

42

since the railroad was built.

September 25, Clark:

> A very hot day. Most of our party complaining and two of
> our hunters left here on the 22nd very sick. They had killed
> only two bucks in my absence. I set out early with the Chief and
> two young men to hunt for trees calculated to build canoes, as
> we had previously determined to proceed on by water.
>
> I was furnished with a horse and we proceeded on down the
> river. Crossed a creek at one mile [Orofino], from the right, very
> rocky, which I call Rock Dam Creek, and passed on down the
> north side of the river to a fork from the north [North Fork],
> which is about the same size and affords about the same quan-
> tity of water with the other fork. We halted about an hour.
>
> One of the young men took his gig and killed six fine salmon.
> Two of them we roasted and ate. Two canoes came up loaded
> with the furniture of two families. These canoes are long, steady
> and without much rake.
>
> I crossed the south fork and proceeded on up the south side,
> the most of the way through a narrow pine bottom in which I
> saw fine timber for canoes.
>
> When I arrived at the camp I found Capt. Lewis and several
> men very sick. I gave some salts and tartar emetic. We deter-
> mined to go to where the best timber was and camp.

Comment: Clark went down the north side of the river from China
Island. He crossed Orofino Creek, which he called Rock Dam Creek.
From there he continued on the north side to where the North Fork
enters the main river. He then crossed the Clearwater River and went
back up the south side to China Island. Notice how numerous the
salmon were in the river.

September 26, Whitehouse:

> Clear and pleasant. We got our horses and set out about 8
> o'clock and proceeded on down the river. Crossed a creek that
> came in on the east side [Orofino], then crossed the river at a
> shoal place, but wide, the water to the horses bellies. Proceeded
> on down the south side of the river and camped opposite of the
> fork which came in on the north side. We formed our camp on
> a narrow plain on the bank of the river. Made a pen of pine
> bushes around the officer's lodge to put all our baggage in. Some
> of the natives followed us with droves of horses.

*Two views from Canoe Camp on the Clearwater River,
the first looking north to the Dworshak Dam in Orofino*

*. . . and the second looking up the Clearwater River from
the public park opposite the fish hatchery.*

> Some came down the North Fork who had been up some distance fishing. Had with them a small raft which they come on with all their baggage, salmon, etc. They run fast on a shoal place about the middle of the river opposite our camp and came out to see us. Some Indians came down from our last night's camp in a canoe with salmon, etc. We went about helving our axes and getting ready to begin the canoes. Several men sick with the relax, caused by a sudden change of diet and water, as well as the climate changed a little also.

Comment: The party came down the north side of the river, crossed Orofino Creek, and then forded the river. This is a long, angling ford which starts just below the present bridge at Orofino and ends at the east end of the airport. This ford was used by the early pioneers before the first bridge was built across the river in 1911.

The place they camped is now called Canoe Camp. It is well marked and there is a fine park there. It is a part of the Nez Perce National Historical Park.

From September 27 to October 4, the party was engaged in digging and burning out the hollows of their canoes. They made four large and one small canoes. In spite of Clark's doctoring, the party got better.

October 5, Clark:

> Wind easterly and cool. Had all our horses, 38 in number, collected and branded. Cut off their foretop and delivered them to the two brothers and one son of one of the chiefs, who intends to accompany us down the river. To each of these men I gave a knife and some small articles. They promised to be attentive to our horses until we should return. . . . Finished and launched two of our canoes this evening, which proved to be very good. Our hunters, with every diligence, could kill nothing.

Comment: Indian legend tells us that the horses were wintered on the hills near Ahsahka. Lewis and Clark found the horses next spring grazing on the ridge between the main river and the North Fork. On October 6, Lewis and Clark buried saddles, a canister of powder, and a bag of musket balls. There is a hole in the hillside near Canoe Camp that Mrs. Holt, a descendant of Twisted Hair, who lived near this place, says according to Indian legend is the cache used by Lewis and Clark. In the spring of 1806, Lewis and Clark state that high water opened their cache and the Indians found it and kept it. I believe the Indians moved the cache to this spot after they found it. Here are some passages that describe where the cache was first located. Clark makes two statements:

> Had a cache made for our saddles and buried them on the side of a pond.

And again:

> . . . had our saddles collected, a hole dug, and in the night buried them, also a canister of powder and a bag of balls, at the place the canoe which Shields made was cut from the body of the tree. The saddles were buried on the side of a bend one half mile below.

Comment: From this description, I place the cache on the flat land, near the river, about one half mile below Canoe Camp. There is a sluggish pond there in the fall of the year.

October 7, Clark:

> I continue very unwell but obliged to attend to everything. All the canoes in the water and loaded. Fixed our canoes as well as possible and set out. As we were about to set out, we missed both of the chiefs who promised to accompany us. I also missed my pipe tomahawk, which could not be found.
>
> The part of the day cloudy. Proceeded on, passed 10 rapids, which were dangerous. The canoe in which I was struck a rock and sprung a leak at the third rapid. We proceed on 20 miles and encamped on a starboard [right] point opposite a run. Passed a small run at 9 miles on the larboard [left] side. A short distance from the river at 2 feet 9 inches, north of a dead topped pine tree, buried two canisters of powder.
>
> Had the canoe unloaded, examined a small leak which was discovered in a thin place in her side. Passed several camps of Indians today. Encamped on a pool to the right.

Comment: When traveling by land, the distances given are accurate and, although it is not stated, someone must have paced the distances. On the water, distances are less accurate. Estimates were no doubt necessary. These were usually too long. The first creek they passed is Canyon Creek and is about six miles. They camped at Lenore, opposite to Jack's Creek. There are no indications of a pond there today. Likely it was filled by railroad construction. This camp is not marked.

Notice that Lewis and Clark made two caches, one near Canoe Camp and one near Lenore. During the winter the Indians found both of these caches and returned them to Lewis and Clark in 1806.

October 8, Whitehouse:

> At about 9 o'clock we set out and proceeded down river. Saw some Indian horses on the hillsides. Passed over several bad rapids. Took some water in the canoes by the waves dashing over the sides. The current rapid the most part of the way, some places deep. Passed cliffs or bare rocks on both sides. About 12 o'clock we came to some Indian camps on the south side, one 4 or 5 lodges of well looking Indians and squaws. They had several small canoes and catch considerable quantities of salmon. We purchased some from them by giving them a few green or blue beads, and tin. The day warm. Some of the men bought two dogs from them. They have a great many horses feeding along the shores and a number of small canoes. A short distance further down two chiefs came with us.
>
> As we were descending a rocky rapids at the foot of an island, on which some Indians were camped, one of the canoes struck a rock and wheeled around, then struck again and cracked the canoe and was near splitting her in two. Threw the steerman [Gass] overboard, who with difficulty got to the canoe again. She soon filled with water and hung on the rocks in a doleful situation. Some of the men on board could not swim, and those that could had no chance for the waves and rocks.
>
> An Indian went out in a small canoe to their assistance. Our little canoe went out also and took out some of the load and carried it to shore. We unloaded one of the other canoes and went into the rapid and took all of the load out of the canoe which was stove. All got to shore below the rapid and camped at dark. Found everything wet which was in the canoe that was stove. Some small articles lost.
>
> A number of natives visit us this evening. We have come about 18 miles this day before the bad experience.

Clark mentions "a creek [Potlatch] falls in on the starboard side one and a half miles above the island." In the return trip he corrects this to one half a mile, which is correct.

Comment: The creek from the right Lewis and Clark called Coulter Creek for John Coulter, a member of their party. It is now Potlatch Creek. The party camped just below Goat Island. There is no marker.

October 9 was spent in drying things and repairing the canoe. Their guide Toby and son suddenly departed without obtaining their pay or letting Lewis or Clark know that they were leaving.

On October 10, Clark's log contains much information of little interest except his description of the country at the mouth of the Clearwater:

> Sixty miles below the forks arrived at a southerly fork which is the one we were on with the Snake or Sosonee nation. . . . The country about the forks is an open plain on either side. I can observe on the lower larboard [left] side a high ridge of thinly timbered country. The water of the south fork [Snake] is greenish blue, the north as clear as crystal. Immediately in the point is an Indian cabin and in the south fork a small island. . . . Worthy of remark that not one stick of timber on the river near the forks, and but few trees for a great way up the river we descended.

Earlier in the day they passed Lapwai Creek with its cottonwoods. Lapwai is a corruption of the Nez Perce word *Lappitwaitash,* meaning boundary, and was the dividing point between the up-river Indians who went to the buffalo country to hunt, and the down-river group, who did not follow this practice. Another interpretation is "the place of butterflies."

[Josiah Pinkham supports "the place of butterfies."]

The Indians call the Snake the *Ki-mo-ie-nem* according to Gass, but there are other spellings. This name means the "river of hemp." The Indians used Indian hemp or dogbane to manufacture rope and gathered much of it along the Snake River. Lewis and Clark called the Salmon and the Snake below where the two rivers joined the Lewis River.

The rest of Lewis and Clark's journey is so far from the Lolo Trail that I will not follow them further west, but will take up their eastward journey.

Chapter 4

LEWIS AND CLARK
The expedition returns in 1806

After wintering at Fort Clatsop, near the mouth of the Columbia River, the Lewis and Clark Expedition started its return journey on March 23, 1806. The trip was by canoe up the Columbia as far as the Dalles. There they purchased some horses and continued to do so at every opportunity, so that in a few days they were traveling entirely by land. They met their old friend, Chief Weahkoonut [Bighorn], with an escort of warriors and arrived on the north side of the Snake River four and a half miles below Lewiston on May 4.

We no longer have a diary by Whitehouse, since he either did not keep one going east, or it cannot be located.

May 5, Lewis:

> Collected our horses and set out at 7 A.M. At four and a half miles we arrived at the entrance of the Kooskooske, up the northwestern side we continue our march . . . passing lodges at 5 to 8 miles above the fork, to a large lodge at 10 miles where, with much difficulty, we obtained two dogs and a small quantity of root bread and dried roots.
>
> At the second lodge we passed, an Indian gave Capt. Clark a very elegant grey mare, for which he requested a phial of eyewater, which was, accordingly given to him. While we were encamped last fall at the mouth of the Chopunnish River [Canoe Camp], Capt. Clark gave an Indian man some volatile linament to rub his knee and thigh for a pain of which he complained, and had not walked for several months. The fellow soon recovered and has never ceased to extol the virtues of our

49

Even today, the Nez Perce country offers tremendous fishing for stealhead and trout.

medicines and the skill of my friend Capt. Clark, as a physician. This occurrence, added to the benefits many of them experienced from the eyewater, has given them an exalted opinion of our medicine. My friend, Capt. Clark, is their favorite physician and has received many applications. In our present situation, I think it pardonable to continue this deception, for they will not give us any provisions and our stock is running low. We take care to give them no article which could possibly injure them.

While at dinner, an Indian fellow very impertinently threw a half starved puppy into my plate, by way of derision for eating dogs, and laughed very heartily at his own impertinence. I was so provoked at his insolence that I caught the puppy and threw it with great violence at him, struck him in the breast and face, seized my tomahawk, and showed him by signs if he repeated his insolence, I would tomahawk him! The fellow withdrew, apparently much mortified, and I continued my repast on dog without further molestation.

After dinner, we continued our route 4 miles to the entrance of Coulter's [Potlatch] Creek, and camped on the lower side. This is one half mile above the rapids where we sank the canoe last fall.

We were a little distance from two lodges. . . . One of these contained eight families and the other was much the largest we have yet seen. It is 156 feet long and about 15 wide, built of mats and straw in the form of the roof of a house. It has a number of small doors on each side, is closed at the ends, without divisions in the interior. This lodge contained at least 30 families.

This is the Chief of one of the four Chiefs of the nation. They call him Nush-ne-pack-ke-ook or Cut Nose, his nose being cut by a lance in battle. To this man we gave a medal of the small size, with a likeness of President Jefferson.

Comment: This was a very interesting day. While eating lunch near Latwai Creek, Lewis had some difficulties over their adopted practice of eating dogs. However, he was probably lucky he restrained his temper and did not kill his offender. The wrath of the tribe might have turned on the party, with disastrous results. On the other hand, Clark, through his kindness and a little medical knowledge, was winning friends and had found a paying practice.

The party came up the north side of the Clearwater and camped at the mouth of Potlatch Creek. There is no marker. A medal, likely the one given to Cut Nose, was uncovered in a grave when the railroad was built past Arrow Junction.

May 6, Lewis:

> This morning the husband of the sick woman was as good as his word. He produced a young horse in tolerable order, which we immediately killed and butchered. The inhabitants seem more accommodating this morning and sold us some bread. We received a second horse for medicine and prescriptions for a little girl with the rheumatism. . . . I exchanged horses with We-ark-koonut and gave him a small flag with which he was much gratified. The sorrel I obtained is an elegant, strong, active, well broken horse. . . . At 3 P.M. we set out accompanied by the brother of Twisted Hair and We-ark-koonut [Big Horn]. We continued our march along the river for 9 miles, to a lodge of six families.

Comment: Clark continues to minister to the sick and earn food for the party. The spelling of Big Horn's name should have been *Weah-Koo-Nut*. There is no sound of "r" in the Nez Perce language, although Lewis and Clark often used it in place of the sound "ah." The Chief was very kind to Lewis. Likely he would have given Lewis the horse without compensation had Lewis so desired.

Lewis and Clark give the color of some fine horses which they received, but never mentioned one that could be considered an Appaloosa.

The party camped at the mouth of Pine Creek. This spot is across the river from the Lewis and Clark Highway, and is unmarked.

May 7, Lewis:

> We collected our horses and set out early, accompanied by the brother of Twisted Hair as a guide. . . . We proceeded up the river 4 miles to a lodge of six families just below the entrance of a small creek [Bedrock]. Here our guide recommended the passing of the river. He informed us that the road was better on the south side and game more abundant. . . . Accordingly, we unloaded our horses and prepared to pass the river, which we effected by means of one canoe in four hours.
>
> A man of this lodge produced us two cannisters of powder which he had found by means of his dog where they had been

buried [near Lenore]. As he kept them safe and had honesty enough to return them, we gave him a fire steel . . . At 3 P.M. we renewed our march along the river about 2 miles, over a difficult stoney road. We then left the river and ascended the hills to the right, which here are mountains high . . . . Our guide conducted us through a plain and down a steep and lengthy hill to a creek [Canyon Creek], which we called Mosquito Creek, the consequence of it being infested with swarms of this insect.

This is a small stream about six yards wide, and heads in the plains at a small distance and discharges into the Kooskooske nine miles by water below the entrance of the Chopunnish River. . . . Ascending the creek on the east side one mile, we arrived at an Indian encampment of six empty lodges. Here we remained all night, having traveled only twelve miles. . . . We saw several deer this evening and a great number of tracks of these animals. We determined to remain here until noon tomorrow in order to obtain some venison. Accordingly, we gave orders to the hunters to turn out early.

The spurs of the mountains which were in view from the high plain were perfectly covered with snow. The Indians inform us that the snow is yet so deep on the mountains that we shall not be able to pass until about the first of June.

Gass, in his diary, states:

We then proceeded over a large hill and struck a small creek about five miles below the place where we made our canoes last October.

Comment: Gass' distance is closer than Lewis' estimate. Most students of Lewis and Clark's travels say that they camped on Jack's Creek. However, the log and their maps clearly show their camp was at or very close to Peck. It is unmarked.

May 8, Lewis:

Most of the hunters turned out by daylight this morning . . . . At about 8 A.M. Shields returned with a small deer, on which we breakfasted. By 11 A.M. all hunters returned. Drewyer and Cruzatte brought each a deer and Collins wounded one, which my dog caught at a little distance from camp. Our stock of provisions now consisted of four deer and the remains of a horse.

We are informed that the natives in this quarter were much distressed for food last winter and were compelled to collect the moss which grows on the pine, which they boiled and ate. Near this camp I observed many pine trees which appear to have been cut down and which they inform us was done in order to collect the seed, which in times of distress furnishes an article of food.

Nush-nu-pah-kee-ook [Cut Nose] and several other Indians joined us this morning. We gave them some venison, horsebeef, and the entrails of four deer and four fawns taken from two of the does. They ate nonè of this food raw, though the entrails had but little preparation and the fawns were boiled and consumed hair, hide and entrails.

These people will sometimes eat horseflesh, though they will, in most instances, suffer extreme hunger before they will kill a horse. This seems rather to proceed from an attachment to this animal, rather than to a dislike to its flesh, as I observe many of them eat heartily on the horsebeef which we give them.

At a half after 3 P.M. we departed for the lodge of Twisted Hair, accompanied by Cut Nose and other Indians. The road led up a steep hill to a high level plain, mostly timbered, through which we passed parrallel with the river about four miles, when we met Twisted Hair and a party of six men. [Here Lewis recounts a quarrel between Cut Nose and Twisted Hair over the care of Lewis and Clark's horses during the past winter.]

To put an end to this dispute, as well to relieve our horses from their loads, we informed the chiefs we should continue our march to the first water and encamp. Accordingly, we moved on about two miles and arrived at a little branch which runs to the right. Here we encamped, having traveled six miles today.

Comment: Lewis and Clark settled the row between the two chiefs. During the day the party climbed the hill east of Peck in a direction parallel to the Clearwater River, about where there is a road today. They went four miles and met Twisted Hair. After going two more miles, they camped on a small creek that goes dry later on in the season but drains into Little Canyon Creek. Since there are so many of these small creeks, I am unable to say just where this camp was located.

May 9, Clark:

We were detained until 9 A.M. for our horses were much scattered; at which time we set out and proceeded on through a beautiful, rich country for six miles to a camp of Twisted Hair. . . . At the distance of two miles, we passed a lodge of two fires on a fork of the road which leads to the right and situated on a small branch which falls into Mosquito [Canyon] Creek.

Soon after we arrived at camp, two boys, with Willard, set out to the river near the place we made the canoes for our saddles and a cannister of powder we buried there. Late in the evening they returned with 21 of the horses and about half of our saddles and the powder and balls.

Comment: This camp of Twisted Hair is now called Wheeler Draw. The Wheeler family were Indians who made their regular home at Ahsahka but used this campground when collecting camas and other roots. There is a spring at this camp, and it was the only permanent water in that locality before the early settlers developed wells.

The Soil Conservation Service constructed a stock pond at this spring. During the construction, according to Ernest Robinson, a pioneer of that locality, they "plowed out a truckload of artifacts." When examining the site, I found numerous flint chips and a pestle for grinding roots.

There is no sign or marker at this camp site. It can be reached only on foot. Anyone trying to locate it should inquire about its location from local ranchers.

May 10, Clark:

This morning the snow continued falling until 6 A.M. when it ceased. We collected our horses and set out . . . proceed on through an open plain. The road slippery, and the snow clogged our horses' feet, causing them to trip frequently . . . At 4 P.M. we arrived at the village of Tin-nach-e-moo-toolt [Broken Arm], with whom we had left a flag. This flag was hoisted on a pole.

Under this flag he met me ... soon after Capt. Lewis, who was in the rear, came up and we smoked with this chief and told him our situation in respect to provisions . . . . We proposed to exchange some of our old horses for young ones to eat. They said they would not exchange horses, but would furnish such as we needed, and produced two, one of which we killed, and reserved the other for a later date.

We gave medals to Broken Arm and Hoh-host-ill-pilp [Red Grizzly Bear]₁₅ . . . The village of Broken Arm consists of one house or lodge 150 feet in length, built of sticks and grass. It contains 24 fires about double that number of families. From

55

appearances, I presume they could raise 100 fighting men. The noise of their women pounding roots reminds me of a nail factory.

Comment: The party has now arrived on Lawyer's Creek. Their meeting with the chiefs was at a place up Lawyer's Creek, one mile above the forks. There is a fish hatchery there now. There is no marker.

On May 11 and 12, the captains talked to the Indians, which was very difficult due to the language barrier. Lewis spoke in English, one of the men translated what he said into French, Charboneau translated it into Minnetaree, Sacajawea translated to Shoshone, and a prisoner translated it to the Nez Perce. Clark was also busy with the sick.

May 13, Lewis:

> This morning Capt. Clark was, as usual, busily engaged with his patients until 11 A.M. At 1 P.M. we collected our horses and set out for the river, escorted by a number of the natives on horseback.
>
> We followed the creek [Lawyer's] downwards about two miles, passing a stout branch [Sevenmile], at one mile which flowed in on the right. We now enter an extensive open bottom through which we pass nearly north about one and a half miles, and halted on the bank of the river at the place appointed to meet the canoe. As the canoe did not arrive until after sunset, we remained here all night.

Comment: The party went down Lawyer's Creek to the end of the canyon, which would be the south edge of Kamiah. From there they went north and camped near the present railroad depot.

Lawyer's Creek is named for Chief Lawyer. Kamiah is pronounced Kam-e-eye today. Lewis and Clark spelled it Cammearp. Substituting "h" for "r" would make it Cammeap. Modern Indians pronounce it *Kame-ahp*. The Indians collected the *kame* or Indian hemp, also called dogbane and manufactured rope, baskets, and mats. As a part of the process, they peeled oft the outer bark and discarded it. Kamiah refers to this trash.

[Ethnographer Josiah Pinkham says the proper spelling of the Nez Perce name for Kamiah is *Qémyexpe*. Indian hemp should be *Qéemu*. Pinkham also notes that, rather than referring to the discarded

Lewis and Clark stayed at their "long camp" beside the Clearwater River from May 15 to June 6, 1806.

outer bark or trash, *Qémyexpe* refers to the prevalence of *Qéemu*, which has declined due to the use of herbicides in agriculture.]

May 14, Lewis:

> After sending out some hunters, transported the baggage by canoe, then drove our horses into the river, over which they swam without accident, although it was 150 yards wide and very rapid.
>
> We then descended the river about a mile and formed our camp on the spot which the Indians had recommended. It was about 40 paces from the river, and formerly an Indian habitation, but nothing remained at present but a circle 30 yards in diameter, sunk in the ground about four feet, with a wall around it about three and a half feet high. In this place we deposited our baggage and around its edges formed our tents of sticks and grass.
>
> This situation is, in many respects, advantageous, It is an extensive, level bottom, thinly covered with long leafed pines, with a rich soil, affording excellent pasture. . . . The high hills on the east and northeast have the best game in the neighborhood, while its vicinity to the river makes it convenient for the salmon, which are expected daily, and have excellent pasture for our horses.

Comment: The Twin Feathers sawmill is now located where Lewis and Clark camped. A part of the old circle [photographed by Wheeler in 1902] was still there until the ground was leveled for the sawmill. This camp is frequently referred to by writers as the "Chopunnish Camp," although Lewis and Clark did not use this name.

From May 15 to June 6 the party was camped at Chopunnish. This is their third longest camp, being exceeded only by winter camps at Mandan and Clatsop.

There are a number of events or passages in the log that are worthy of note. The dress of the Nez Perces as described by Lewis is interesting:

> They are generally well clothed in their style. Their dress consists of a long skirt which reaches to the middle of the thigh, tong leggings that reach as high as the waist, mocassins, and robes. These are formed of various skins and are in all respects like those of the Shoshonees.
>
> Their ornaments consist of beads, shells, and pieces of brass, variously attached to their dress, to their ears, around their necks, wrists, and arms. A band of some kind usually surrounds the head. This is, most frequently, of the skin of some fur animal, as fox or otter, although they also have them of dressed skin without the hair.
>
> The ornament of the nose is a single shell of wampum. Pearl and beads are suspended from the ears. The hair is queued in two rolls, which hang on each side in front of the shoulders. Collars of bear claws are common, but the article on which they bestow most pains and ornaments is a kind of collar or breastplate. This is commonly a piece of otter skin about six inches wide, taken out of the center of the skin, its whole length including the head. This is dressed with the hair on. A hole is cut lengthwise through the skin near the head of the animal sufficiently large to permit the head of the person to pass. Then it is placed about the neck and hangs in front of the body, the tail frequently reaching below the knees. On the front of this skin are attached pieces of pearl, beads, wampum, pieces of red cloth, and, in short, whatever they conceive most valuable or ornamental.
>
> I observed a tippet worn by Hohastiliplip, which was formed of human scalps and ornamented with the thumbs and fingers of several men which he had slain in battle.

Notice that the Nez Perce Indians did pierce their noses and take scalps, facts later often denied.

[Ethnographer Josiah Pinkham asserts that the people seen by Lewis are actually individuals from the Lower Columbia River who married into the Nez Perce Tribe. That the Nez Perce pierced their noses is a myth that has been perpetuated for generations.]

Another interesting thing brought out in the journals is that grizzly bears were quite common on the ridge between the Clearwater River and Lolo Creek. This animal disappeared from the Clearwater country many years ago. [Publisher's note: The last verified death of a grizzly bear in this ecosystem took place in 1932. However, beginning in 2002 or 2003, the U.S. Fish and Wildlife Service has recommended the reintroduction of twenty-five grizzlies into the six-thousand-square-mile Bitterroot Grizzly Bear Recovery Area within the Selway-Bitterroot and Frank Church-River of No Return Wilderness Areas, south of the Lolo Trail.] Another change in wildlife is in the elk population. Lewis and Clark did not kill an elk in their stay and did not mention seeing a track until they were near Powell on their return east.

While camped near Kamiah, members of the party covered a rather large area in search of food. Sergeant Ordway even went to the Salmon River and down it to its junction with the Snake. The fish he brought back had spoiled.

The Nez Perce Indians claim that Capt. Clark had a son born of a Nez Perce woman[16]. Indian legend says this woman was a sister of Chief Red Grizzly. This son had red or yellow hair and was proud of his ancestry. He would straighten his body to its full height and strike his chest, exclaiming as he did so, "Me Clark." He joined with Joseph, was taken prisoner, and died in Kansas. However, he had a daughter, Mary Clark, who lived on the Flathead Indian Reservation in Montana.

There is a story among the Nez Perce that a black baby was also born to a Nez Perce woman after the Lewis and Clark party left, but this child died before reaching maturity.

Of course, there is no way to prove or disprove these statements, but a red- or yellow-haired Indian does point at Clark. The diaries of

Logging and agriculture make up much of the economy of Weippe Prairie today.

the Captains and the men say nothing about such possibilities among the Nez Perce. Elsewhere they state, "our men found no difficulty in procuring companions for the night" and "a curious custom with the Sioux and Ricara is to give handsome squaws to those they wish to show more acknowledgments to."

June 10, Clark:

> We arose early and had all our horses collected except one of Whitehouse's, which could not be found. An Indian prom-ised to find the horse and bring him to us at the quamash fields [Weippe Prairie], at which place we intend to delay a few days to lay in some meat, by which time we calculate the snows will be melted off the mountains and the grass raised to a sufficient height for our horses to live.
>
> We packed up and set out at 11 A.M., each man being well mounted and a light load on a second horse. Besides these, we have several supernumerary horses in case of accident, or want of provisions. We, therefore, feel ourselves perfectly equipped for the mountains.
>
> We ascend the hills, which are very high and about three miles in extent, our course being N 22 E, thence N 15 W, two miles to Collins [Lolo] Creek, thence five miles north to the eastern borders of the quamash flats, where we encamped near the place I first met with the Chopunnish last fall.
>
> The pass of Collins Creek was deep and extremely difficult, though we passed without further injury than wetting some of our roots and bread.
>
> The country through which we passed is extremely fertile and generally free from stone, is well timbered with several species of fir, pine and larch.
>
> After we encamped this evening we sent out our hunters. Collins killed a doe, on which we supped, much to our satisfac-tion. We find a great number of burrowing squirrels about our camp, of which we killed several. I ate of them and found them quite as tender and well flavored as our grey squirrel. Saw many sand hill cranes and some ducks in the glades about this place.

Lewis locates their camp as follows:

> Our camp is agreeably situated in a point of timber land on the eastern border of an extensive, level and beautiful prairie, which is intersected by several small branches, near the bank of one of which our camp is placed. The quamash is in full bloom

and at a short distance resembles lakes of fine, clear water.

Comment: Thanks to the generosity of the Nez Perce Indians, the Lewis and Clark party is now well-equipped with good horses.

Lewis and Clark went over the old trail from Kamiah to Weippe. The present road follows close to the old trail.

Lewis and Clark camped near where the Opresik house now stands. The land all around this house is now farmed, but when I was a boy a grove of pine ran up the low ridge between two branches of Fords Creek.

Lewis and Clark mention quamash or camas many times, for it was one of the principal foods of the Indians. There are two kinds of edible camas in the Clearwater country. One has a blue and the other a purple blossom. The Indians much preferred the blue colored camas, which grew in abundance on all the meadows in the Weippe country. Further north in Idaho the purple camas is dominant and I was surprised to find that the camas at Packer Meadows is the purple variety.

The party spent June 11 to 14 at Weippe Prairie hunting with moderate success.

June 15, Clark:

> Collected our horses early with intention of making an early start. Some hard showers detained us until 10 A.M., at which time we took our final departure from the quamash flats [Weippe prairie] and proceeded with much difficulty, due to the slippery road. At nine miles we passed a small prairie [Crane Meadows] in which was quamash. At two miles further we are at the camp of Fields and Willard on Collins Creek. They arrived at this creek last evening and killed another deer near the creek.
>
> Here we let our horses graze in a small glade and ate dinner. [This is the so-called Wolf Camp on Lolo Creek]. After detaining about two hours, we proceed on, passing the creek three times and passing over some rugged hills and spurs, passing the creek on which I camped Sept. 17 [Cedar Creek]. [Clark is in error. This should be Sept. 19.] Came to a small glade of about 10 acres thickly covered with grass and quamash near a creek [Eldorado] and encamped.
>
> We passed through bad fallen timber and a high mountain

this evening. From the top of this mountain I had an extensive view of the rocky mountains to the south and the Columbia Plains for a great extent. Also in the S.W. a range of high mountains which divides the Lewis and Clark rivers [Salmon and Snake]. Several high points to the N. and N.E. covered with snow. A remarkable high rugged mountain [Seven Devils] in the forks of Lewis and Clark rivers covered with snow.

Comment: The party left Weippe Prairie and at Crane Meadows found two deer killed by their hunters. They then overtook the hunters at Lolo Creek. They then traveled to Eldorado Creek and camped at the meadows at the mouth of Lunch Creek.

Apparently the ridge between Cedar and Eldorado Creeks had been burned over, because Clark complained of windfalls. Also, Clark was able to view the surrounding country much better than you can from this point today.

The Columbia Plains he wrote about are, of course, the Nez Perce and Camas Prairies. The high mountains between the Snake and Salmon Rivers are the Seven Devils. The mountains to the north and northwest are Bald Mountain and Hemlock Butte.

June 16, Lewis:

We collected our horses very early this morning, took breakfast and set out at 6 P.M. Proceed up the creek [Eldorado] about two miles through some handsome meadows of fine grass, abounding with quamash. Here we passed the creek [Eldorado] and ascended a ridge which led us to the N.E. about seven miles, when we arrived at a small branch of Hungry Creek [actually a branch of Fish Creek]. The difficulty we met with fallen timber detained us so much we arrived at 11 A.M. Here is a handsome little glade in which we found some grass for our horses. We, therefore, halted to let them graze and took dinner, knowing there was no other place suitable for that purpose short of the glades on Hungry Creek, where we intend to camp.

Before we reached this little branch on which we dined, we saw in the hollows and north hillsides large quantities of snow. In some places two feet deep. . . However, we determined to proceed. Accordingly after taking a hearty meal, we continue our route through a thick wood with much fallen timber and intersected by many small ravines and high hills.

The snow increased in quantity so much that the greater

part of our route this evening was over snow, which has become sufficiently firm to bear our horses. Otherwise it would have been impossible to pass, as it lay in masses, in some places 8 or 10 feet deep. We had much difficulty in pursuing the road, as it was so frequently covered with snow.

We arrived early at the place that Capt. Clark had killed and left the flesh of a horse for us last September. Here is a small glade in which there was some grass. Not a sufficiency for our horses, but we thought it most advisable to remain here all night, as we anticipate if we proceed further we should find less grass . . . We came 15 miles today.

Comment: The party proceeded up Eldorado Creek, crossed it and then up the ridge between Dollar and Sixbit Creeks, over the main divide into the drainage of Fish Creek, where they found a small meadow and lunched. They then went over another divide into Hungry Creek and camped at a small meadow. This meadow is unmarked, but it is just below Windy Saddle on the road to Boundary Peak.

June 17, Clark:

We collected our horses and set out early. We proceeded down Hungry Creek about 7 miles, passing it twice. We found it difficult and dangerous to pass the creek in consequence of its depth and rapidity. We avoided two passes of the creek by ascending a steep, rocky and difficult hill.

Beyond the creek, the road ascends the mountains to the height of the main ridges, which divides the waters of the Kooskooske [Lochsa] and Chopunnish [North Fork] rivers. This morning we ascended about 3 miles, when we found ourselves enveloped in snow from 8 to 12 feet deep, even on the south side of the mountains.

I was in front and could only pursue the direction of the road by the trees which had been peeled by the natives for the inner bark, which they scrape and eat. As these trees were scattered, I, with great difficulty, pursued the direction of the road one mile further to the top of the mountain, where I found snow from 12 to 15 feet deep. Here was winter with all its rigors. The air was cold and my hands and feet benumbed.

We knew it would require four days to reach the fish weir at the entrance of Colt Killed Creek [Whitesand], provided we were so fortunate as to be able to follow the proper ridge of mountains to lead us there. Of this all of our most expert woodsmen

The signpost indicates that you can get to a lot of destinations from the old gold-mining town of Pierce, Idaho (left), while nearby residents (below) enjoy their privacy.

and experienced guides were extremely doubtful. Short of that point, we could not hope for any food for our horses.

If we proceeded and should get bewildered in these mountains, the certainty was that we should lose all of our horses and consequently our baggage, instruments, perhaps our papers, and then eventually risk the loss of our discoveries which we had already made, if we should be so fortunate to escape with life . . Under these circumstances, we decided it madness in this stage of the expedition to proceed without a guide.

We, therefore, came to the resolution to return with our horses while they were yet strong and in good order, and endeavor to keep them so until we could procure an Indian to conduct us over the snowy mountains. Having come to this resolution, we ordered the party to make a deposit of our baggage which we did not have an immediate use for; also the roots, bread or cowis which they had, except an allowance for a few days to enable them to return to a place at which we could subsist by hunting until we obtained a guide.

We left our instruments and I left most of my papers, believing them safer here than to risk them on horseback over the road which we had passed.

Our baggage being on scaffolds and well covered, we began our retrograde march at 1 P.M., having remained about 3 hours on the snowy mountain. We returned by the route we advanced from Hungry Creek which we ascended about two miles and encamped. . . . The party was a good deal dejected, though not as much as I had anticipated.

Comment: The mountain on which the baggage was deposited is just west of Sherman Saddle and although it is unnamed on the map it is locally known as Willow Ridge. Their camp was on the south side of Hungry Creek. It is marked with an iron post driven in the ground.

June 18, Clark:

This morning we had considerable difficulty in collecting our horses, they having straggled off to a considerable distance in search of food on the sides of the mountain in the thick timber. A 9 o'clock we collected them all except two, one of which was Shield's and one of Drewyer's. We set out leaving Shields and LePage to collect the two horses and follow us.

We dispatched Drewyer and Shannon to the Chopunnish Indians in the plains beyond the Kooskooske in order to hasten the arrival of the Indians who promised to accompany us, or to procure a guide at all events, and rejoin us as soon as possible. We sent by them a rifle, which we offered as a reward to any of them who would engage to conduct us to Clark's [Bitterroot] River at the entrance of Travelers Rest [Lolo] Creek. We also directed them, if they found difficulty in inducing any of them to accompany us, to offer the reward of two other guns to be given them immediately, and ten horses at the falls of the Missouri [Great Falls, Montana].

We had not proceeded far this morning before J. Potts cut his leg very badly with one of the large knives. He cut one of the large veins on the inner side of the leg.

Colter's horse fell with him in crossing Hungry Creek. He and his horse were carried down the creek a considerable distance, rolling over each other among the rocks. He fortunately escaped without much injury or the loss of his gun. He lost his blanket.

At 1 P.M. we arrived at the glade where we dined on the 16th. Here we again halted and dined. As there were some appearance of deer about this place we left J. and R. Fields with directions to hunt this evening and tomorrow morning at this place and join us tomorrow evening at the meadows on Collins [Lolo] Creek, where we intend to stay tomorrow to rest and hunt.

After dinner we proceeded on to the near fork of Collins Creek [Eldorado] and encamped in a pleasant situation at the upper part of the meadows about two miles above our encampment of June 15. We sent out several hunters, but they returned without killing anything. They saw a number of large fish in the creek and shot at them several times without success. We ordered Gibson and Colter to prepare giggs in the morning and endeavor to take some of the fish. The hunters saw much fresh appearance of bear, but very little deer sign. We hope by means of the fish and what deer and bear we kill to subsist until our guide arrives, without the necessity of returning to the quamash flat [Weippe]. There is a great abundance of food here to sustain our horses . . . . Mosquitoes troublesome.

Comment: The party retraced its route to Eldorado Creek and camped at the mouth of Dollar Creek. The present Forest Service road crosses Eldorado Creek at this point. The Forest Service has a marker planned for this site.

The mosquitoes at Eldorado Meadows come after you in swarms in the spring of the year. I don't see how they endured them.

Because of the snow, it was late June before the expedition made it to the heights of the Lolo Trail.

There is a falls in Eldorado Creek near its mouth. Today, the steelhead cannot go above the falls, and I am surprised that they made it above the falls in 1806.

The party stayed at Eldorado Meadows June 19 and 20 hunting, fishing, and fighting mosquitoes. Hunting was poor so they decided to return to Weippe Prairie. The lost horses were not found.

On June 21, the party returned to Weippe and "found ourselves at our old encampment." They met two Indians en route who had part of their lost stock, which included a mule.

June 22 and 23 were spent at Weippe hunting with very good success. At 3 P.M. on the second day, Shannon and Drewyer returned with three Choppunnish guides.

June 24, Lewis:

> We collected our horses early this morning and set out, accompanied by our three guides. . . . We nooned it at Collins [Lolo] Creek . . . . After dinner we continued our route to Fish [Eldorado] Creek, a branch of Collins [Lolo] Creek, where we

had lain on the 19 and 20th [mouth of Dollar Creek]. We had fine grass for our horses this evening.

Comment: With food, good horses and three expert Nez Perce guides, they were ready to make a second assault on their much feared foe, the Bitterroot Mountains. Notice in the next few days that these guides never miss. They waste no time looking for the trail and camp with horsefeed every night. It is unfortunate that none of those who kept diaries gave the names of their Nez Perce guides. Some Indians say one of the guides was a son of Twisted Hair and another the son of Red Grizzly.

June 25, Lewis:

> Last evening the Indians entertained us by setting the fir trees on fire. They place a great number of dried limbs near the trunk, which when set on fire creates a very sudden and immense blaze from bottom to top of these tall trees. They are beautiful in this situation at night. This exhibition reminded me of a display of fireworks. The natives told us that their object in setting the trees on fire was to bring fair weather for our journey.
>
> We collected our horses at an early hour this morning. One of our guides complained of being unwell, a symptom I did not much like, as such complaints with an Indian is generally the prelude to his abandoning any enterprise with which he is not well pleased. We left them at our encampment and they promised to pursue us in a few hours.
>
> At 11 A.M. we arrived at the branch of Hungry Creek, where we found R. and J. Fields. They had not killed anything. Here we halted and dined and our guides overtook us. [This is the third time they nooned it here.] After dinner we continued our route to Hungry Creek and encamped about one and a half miles below our camp of June 16.
>
> The Indians continue with us and I believe are disposed to be faithful to their engagements. I gave the sick Indian a buffalo robe, he having no other covering except his mocassins and a dressed elk skin without the hair.
>
> Drewyer and Shields were sent on this morning to Hungry Creek in search of their horses, which they fortunately recovered.

Comment: Being a retired forester and firefighter I cannot help

The Nez Perce prayed at the "smoking place," while Lewis marveled at "these stupendeous mountains."

wondering how far the fires the Indians set spread during the follow-ing summer.

To start a journey of the Bitterroots at this time of year clothed only in moccasins and an elk skin was certainly poor judgment, and it is small wonder the guide became ill. Apparently Lewis' assistance solved the problem and retained their guides.

[Ethnographer Josiah Pinkham disagrees with the author's sup-position that this was poor judgement. Nez Perce men accustomed themselves to the cold. They frequently took cold water baths even in the winter when they would have to break through the river's ice. They did this to strengthen their bodies and minds.]

Their camp today was on a small meadow on Hungry Creek. It may be this meadow was off the old trail because it was not men-tioned before. The guides would know about it.

June 26, Lewis:

This morning we collected our horses and set out after an early breakfast, or at 6 A.M. We passed by the same route we had traveled on the 17th to our deposit on the top of the snowy mountain to the N.E. of Hungry Creek. Here we halted two hours to arrange our baggage and prepare our loads. We cooked and ate a hasty meal of boiled venison and cowis.

The snow has subsided near four feet since the 17th. We now measured it accurately and found from a mark we had made on a tree when we were last here on the 17th that it was then 10 feet 10 inches, which appeared to be about the common depth, though it is deeper still in some places. It is now generally about 7 feet.

On our way up this mountain we killed two of the small black pheasants [fool hens or Franklin grouse] and a female of the larger dominecker or speckled pheasant [blue grouse] . . . The Indians inform us that neither of these species drum. They ap-pear to be very silent birds, for I have never heard any of them make a noise in any situation.

The Indians hasten to be off and informed us that it was a considerable distance to the place which they wished to reach this evening, where there was grass for our horses. Accordingly we set out with our guides, who led us over and along the steep sides of tremendous mountains entirely covered with snow, except about the roots of trees, where the snow had sometimes melted and exposed a few square feet of earth.

We ascended and descended several lofty heights, but keeping on the dividing ridge between the Kooskooske [Lochsa] and Chopunnish [North Fork] rivers, we passed no stream of water. Late in the evening, much to our satisfaction and the comfort of our horses, we arrived at the desired spot and encamped on the steep side of a mountain convenient to a good spring. There we found an abundance of fine grass for our horses. This situation was the side of an untimbered mountain with a fair southern aspect, where the snows, from appearance, had been dissolved about 10 days. The grass was young and tender, of course, and had much the appearance of a lawn.

Comment: The Indians were correct. Neither the Franklin or blue grouse drums. But they do make noises. During the mating season the male blue grouse makes a grunting sound, or ump-ump-ump. The fool hen makes a snapping noise while strutting. The female of both species call their young by clucking sounds.

The party camped at Bald Mountain, which has been a favorite camping ground for parties traveling the Lolo Trail, due to its abundant grass. The Nez Perce call this *kount keaut* meaning bare hill.

The spring of 1806 must have been unusually late. The snow is usually gone at this time of year except in drifts and shaded places.

June 27, Lewis:

We collected our horses and set out. The road still continued on the heights of the same dividing ridge on which we traveled yesterday for 9 miles to our camp of Sept. 17. About one mile short of this camp, on an elevated point, we halted by the request of the Indians a few minutes to smoke the pipe.

On this point the natives have raised a conic mound of stones of six or eight feet high, and on its summit erected a pine pole 15 feet long. From thence, they inform us, that passing over with their families some of the men were usually sent on foot by the fishery at the entrance of Colt Creek, [Whitesand], in order to take fish and again meet the main party at the Quamash Glade [Packer Meadow] at the head of the Kooskooske River.

From this place we had an extensive view of the stupendeous mountains, principally covered with snow like that on which we stood. We were entirely surrounded by these mountains, from which, to one unacquainted with them, it would have

In several places where the Motorway leaves the Old Trail, hikers and horsemen can follow the explorers' path.

seemed impossible ever to have escaped. In short, without the assistance of our guides, I doubt much whether we, who once passed them, could find our way to Travelers' Rest Creek [Lolo, Montana]. These fellows are most remarkable pilots. We find the road wherever the snow has disappeared, though it be only for a few paces.

After smoking the pipe and contemplating this scene . . . we continued our march, and at the distance of three miles, descended a steep mountain and passed two small branches of the Chopunnish River just above their forks, and again ascended the ridge on which we passed several miles, and at a distance of 7 miles arrived at our encampment of Sept. 16, near which we passed 3 small branches of the Chopunnish River and again ascending the dividing ridge, on which we continue 9 miles, when the ridge becoming lower and we arrived at a station very similar to our encampment of last evening, though the ridge was somewhat higher and the snow had not been so long disolved. Of course, there was little grass. Here we encamped for the night, having traveled 28 miles over these mountains without relieving our horses from their packs or their having food.

The Indians inform us that there are, in the mountains to our left, an abundance of mountain sheep, or what they call white buffalo [mountain goats]. We saw three mule deer this evening but were unable to get a shot at them. We also saw several tracks of these animals in the snow.

The Indians inform us that there is a great abundance of elk in the valley about the fishery of the Kooskooske River.

Our meat being exhausted, we issued a pint of bears oil to a man, which with their boiled roots, made an agreeable dish.

Pott's leg, which has been swollen and inflamed for several days, is much better this evening and gives him but little pain.

Comment: The rock mound on which the Indians stopped to smoke was located on the first high point west of Indian Grave. It is off the Lolo Motorway but on the Old Lolo Trail. [Publisher's note: Visitors can walk along the Old Trail beginning at here two-and-a-half miles to the Sinque Hole.] There is a small rock mound there now, much smaller than the one Lewis described. It could be the same mound much settled, or it may be that another one was erected. There are a number of old rock mounds along the Lolo Trail.

If you aren't walking or riding your horse, the Old Lolo Trail is closed.

Notice that the trail Lewis and Clark followed left the main divide and dropped down on the north side to the forks of Gravey and Serpent Creeks. It then climbed onto the ridge north of Howard Creek, then crossed Howard and Moose Creeks, and came back to the main divide near or at Indian Post Office. They camped at Spring Hill and their campsite has a Forest Service marker. The Nez Perce called this *Mansum llppilp* [Proper spelling *mêxsem 'ilp 'ilp*] or Red Mountain for the dock on it which turns red in the fall.

The mountains to the northeast where the Indians hunted mountain goats is the Rhodes Peak country. There are goats there today.

Apparently elk were plentiful in the country around Powell Ranger Station. Likely the Indians hunted around the Colgate and Jerry Johnson Warm Springs. When I first visited Colgate Warm Springs in 1924, there was a platform built in a large cedar tree where hunters could lay in wait for game.

As to the agreeable dish of roots and bear's oil, ugh!

June 28, Clark:

> This morning we collected our horses and set out early as usual, after an early breakfast. We continued our route along the dividing ridge over knobs and deep hollows. Passed our camp of Sept. 14 last near the forks of the road, leaving the road on which we had come, one leading to the fishery on our right immediately on the dividing ridge.
>
> At 12 o'clock we arrived at an untimbered hillside of a mountain with a southern aspect just above the fishery. Here we found an abundance of grass for our horses, as our guide had informed us. As our horses were hungry and much fatigued and from our information no other place where we could obtain grass for them within the reach of this evening's travel, we decided to remain at this place all night, having come 13 miles only.

Comment: Gass adds that they saw numerous elk tracks at this campground. This is the only time elk tracks are mentioned in the Clearwater Valley.

The party has taken a shorter route than their westward journey and has arrived at Powell Junction near the place where the road goes to Rocky Point Lookout. This camp is marked only with an iron post.

June 29, Clark:

> We collected our horses early and set out, having previously dispatched Drewyer and R. Fields to warm springs [Lolo Hot Springs] to hunt. We pursued the heights of the ridge on which we have been passing for several days. It terminated at the distance five miles from our camp and we descended to and passed the main branch of the Kooskooske [Crooked Creek] one and a half miles above the entrance of Glade [Brushy] Creek, which falls in on the N. E. side. When we descended from the ridge we bid adieu to the snow.
>
> Near the river we found a deer which the hunters had killed and left us. This was a fortunate supply, as our oil was now exhausted and we were reduced to our roots alone, without salt. The Kooskooske [Crooked Fork] at this place is about 30 yards wide and runs with great velocity. The bed, as of all the mountain streams, is composed of smooth stones.
>
> Beyond the river we ascend a very steep mountain about

two miles, and arrive at the summit, where we found the old trail by which we passed when we went west, coming in from our right. The road was now much plainer and more beaten, which, we were informed, happened from Ootshashoots [Flatheads] visiting the fishery frequently from the valley of the Clark's [Bitterroot] River, though there was no appearance of their having been here this spring.

At noon we arrived at the quamash flats and halted to graze our horses and dine, having traveled 12 miles. We passed our camp of Sept. 13 at 10 miles. We halted at a pretty little plain of about 50 acres, plentifully stocked with quamash and from appearances this forms one of the principal stages or encampments of Indians who pass the mountains on this road.

After dinner we continued our march 7 miles to the warm springs where we arrived early in the evening and sent out several hunters. [Here the warm springs are described. The party, including the guides, bathes in the warm water.]

Comment: The ridge they were following ended at Rocky Point, and they descended to and crossed the Crooked Fork. They then climbed the ridge to the southeast and came to their old trail, which they followed to Packer Meadows, lunching at the eastern edge. They then went to Lolo Hot Springs and camped. A Forest Service sign now marks this camp. There is also a restaurant and other facilities there to accommodate travelers. [Publisher's Note: Visitors can still bathe in the hot springs, now a commercial endeavor with a full-sized pool. A newly built motel and an RV campground make Lolo Hot Springs a good jumping off point for traveling the Lolo Trail.]

June 30, Clark:

We dispatched Drewyer and J. Fields early this morning ahead to hunt. Just as we prepared to set out, a deer came to lick at the springs and one of our hunters killed it. This secured our dinner.

We proceeded down the creek, sometimes in the bottoms and at other times on the tops or along the steep sides, to the north of the creek. At one and a half miles we passed our camp of Sept. 12. We nooned at a place we had on the 12 of September. While here, Shields killed a deer on the North Fork near the road that leads up the North Fork [Graves Creek]. Here a road leads up the North Fork and passes over to an extensive valley on the Clark's River. [The Clark Fork River near Alberton.]

Soon after setting out Shields killed another deer and we picked up 3 more which Drewyer had killed on the road. Deer are very abundant in the neighborhood of Travelers' Rest [Lolo], also some big horn and elk.

A little before sunset we arrived at our camp on the south side of the creek [Lolo], a little above its entrance into Clark's Fork [Bitterroot].

Here we encamp with a view to remain two days in order to rest ourselves and horses and make final arrangements for separation.

Comment: The party is now back at the old camp on Travelers' Rest or Lolo Creek, near Lolo, Montana. Here they bid farewell to their Nez Perce guides, whom they considered, with good reason, the best of friends. Gass says of the Nez Perces:

It is but justice to say that the whole nation to which they belong are the most friendly, honest, and ingenious people that we have seen in the course of our voyage and travels. After taking our farewell of these good hearted, hospitable and obliging sons of the west, we proceeded on. . . .

At Lolo the party split in two, Captain Clark going up the Bitterroot and Lewis up the Blackfoot Rivers.

Chapter 5

JOHN WORK
The Hudson Bay Party

By 1831 the competition between the Hudson's Bay Company and the American fur traders for the fur trade had become quite keen. This was especially true in Montana, Wyoming, and Colorado. To challenge the American companies in this area, John Work—or John Walk— left the Hudson's Bay post at Vancouver, just across the Columbia River from Portland in the fall of 1831.

His party of between thirty-five and sixty men, women, and children included his wife and three daughters. The party reached Weippe on September 26, 1831. There were Indians at Weippe, and Work attempted to trade with them. They found the Nez Perce not interested in beaver trapping and hard bargainers when it came to trading horses.

On September 30 they moved to a "little valley . . the country here has been burned and is pretty bare of wood." This, in my opinion, was Brown's Creek, although some consider it Musselshell. My opinion is based on the age of the timber. The timber at Musselshell before harvest in the 1950s was over two hundred years old; that at Brown's Creek about one hundred and thirty.

On October 1, Work wrote, "It began to snow in the night and snowed all day." It is unusual for snow on October 1 at this elevation, but not for the Lolo Trail.

On October 2 the party started over the Lolo Trail and made twenty-four miles "over very steep hills and thick woods" and "encamped in a deep valley." Here there was no grass and the horses ate "bramble and briars. We have now fallen on the great road."

Some say this camp was at Deep Saddle and the description would fit except for the statement that they had reached the "great road." This would have to be the trail as followed by Lewis and Clark, and that makes it Sherman Saddle since the trail followed by Lewis and Clark turned down into Hungry Creek on the ridge west of Sherman Saddle.

There are no clues as to where the trail followed by Work ran but apparently it was close to the Lolo Trail as established by Bird in 1866.

On October 3 the party made seventeen miles through nine inches of snow and camped by grass. This puts them at Bald Mountain.

Storms prevented travel on October 4. They spent the day looking for missing horses.

More snow fell on October 5. The party moved fifteen miles, which puts them at Camp Howard. The grass was covered with snow "so the starving horses could not get it."

On October 6 the snow continued, and more horses were lost. One horse died, another "gave up." Their camp appears to be at Cayuse Junction. There is no horse feed at Cayuse Junction.

Stragglers catching up with the main party reported six feet of snow on the higher elevations to the west on October 7. This would be at Indian Post Office and Spring Hill. Work reported less than a foot of snow at the camp site.

On October 8 the snow turned to rain as they moved to lower elevation. They made fifteen miles and camped on the Crooked Fork. Again, no horse feed.

The next day they managed eight miles and reached Packer Meadows. "There is a good deal of good grass for the horses, of which they are in much need," Work wrote. They camped for three days to rest themselves and give their horses an opportunity to feed on good grass.

On October 13 they moved to "a small plain at a hot spring." This is Lolo Hot Springs.

Thus the second known white party crossed the Lolo Trail. They found it just as difficult as their predecessors, Lewis and Clark. Work's mission was not a success. He could not compete with the prices offered for furs by the "Boston man." He returned to Vancouver by way of south Idaho.

Chapter 6

CAPTAIN JOHN MULLAN, U.S. ARMY
Looking for a Good Place for a Road

Captain John Mullan explored the possibilities of constructing a military road from Walla Walla, Washington, to Fort Benton in Montana.

His field examination started in 1853 and was completed in 1854. He first interviewed the Indians, hunters, trappers, and priests who had traveled the country. He soon learned that a route from Fort Benton to Missoula was not difficult, and, in March 1854, he brought a wagon over this route, reaching the Missoula Valley on March 31, 1854. This narrowed his explorations down to finding a route from Missoula to Walla Walla, which was not easy.

He explored all possible routes going over the Lolo Trail in September 1854. The following quote is from his 1863 report:

> In September 1854, my party having been ordered in from the field, I determined to proceed to the coast by a new route, and the only one left unexplored, namely, via the Lo-Lo Fork Pass; not that I felt or believed it to be practicable for wagons, but more with a view to arm my judgment with such facts as would not leave a shadow of a doubt behind which would cause us to error in the final conclusion in so important a matter. This route I found the most difficult of all examined. After eleven days of severe struggle with climate and country we emerged into the more open region where "Oro Fino" now stands, glad to leave behind us so difficult a bed of mountains. After examining all these passes my judgment was finally decided in favor

of the line, via the Coeur d'Alene Pass, as a proper connection for a road leading from the head of navigation on the Columbia to that on the Missouri, and the result was so reported to Governor Stevens, under whose direction I was then acting.

The three principal routes examined by Captain Mullan were the Clark Fork, St. Regis to Coeur d'Alene, and Lolo Pass. The Northern Pacific Railroad and Highway 10 North now follow the Clark Fork River route, and Highway 12 now goes through Lolo Pass.

[Publisher's Note: Interstate 90 now follows the St. Regis cutoff to Coeur d'Alene, while U.S. Highway 200 follows the Clark Fork River, and U.S. Highway 12 goes through Lolo Pass and links Missoula, Montana to Lewiston, Idaho.]

Considering the road-building equipment of the time, no doubt Mullan picked the most practical route.

Notice that the name Lo-Lo was well established in 1854. The Oro Fino of 1863 was not the Orofino of today, but a mining town close to the present town of Pierce.

Some western sections of the Lolo Trail were rebuilt as a road by Wellington Bird, an Iowa engineer, in 1866.

Chapter 7

WELLINGTON BIRD AND MAJOR TRAUX
Rerouting the Trail

G old was discovered at Pierce late in 1860 and a rush to the gold fields of the Clearwater took place in 1861. At first Walla Walla was the base of operations, but a town was soon established at Lewiston, which then served as the taking off point and supply center.

[This rush to the gold fields was a breach of the 1855 treaty between the United States and the Nez Perce.]

Gold was found at Elk City and Florence, Idaho, and then in 1863 the big find was made at Alder Gulch in what is now Virginia City, Montana.

The base of supplies for Virginia City was Salt Lake City, Utah. Lewiston tried to get in on the trade and some men, such as Lloyd Magruder, took supplies to Virginia City by pack train, going over the Nez Perce Trail. But Salt Lake City had a distinct advantage over Lewiston because freight could be hauled from there by wagon.

The long and short of it is that the merchants of Lewiston promoted a wagon road east by way of Lolo Pass. There was a road to Pierce, Idaho, and they reasoned that it would be practical to make a shorter route to Montana by building a road through the mountains to Missoula.

Pressure was brought on Congress to build such a road and in 1865 Congress—always in favor of promoting development of the west—appropriated $50,000 to construct a road over Lolo Pass. Little did anyone realize the difficulties involved. It was 74 years before this road was completed.

Although the appropriation was made in 1865, the Secretary of Interior could not find a competent engineer to undertake the job. The pay was $2,000 per year, a fair sum in the East but not much in Idaho Territory in 1865, where prices and wages were much higher.

In 1866 the government hired Wellington Bird, an Iowa engineer, as the Chief Engineer and George B. Nicholson as his assistant. Professor Oliver Marcy, a botanist and zoologist, from Northwestern University, accompanied the party.

Bird's original plan was to assemble an outfit in the east and move it west to Lewiston, but after consultation with the Secretary of the Interior he discarded this idea and took passage on March 10, 1866, by boat to Portland, Oregon.

At Portland, Bird and his aides bought some road building equipment. They then moved to Lewiston, arriving on May 1, 1866. At Lewiston Bird spent considerable time talking to people about the geography of the country and making final preparations for an assault on the Lolo Trail.

The party left Lewiston on May 24. It was a sizeable outfit consisting of Wellington Bird and George Nicholson, engineers; Oliver Marcy, scientist; Major Sewell Truax, one time commander of Fort Lapwai, surveyor; Col. William Craig, the first white settler in Idaho, who had a ranch near the present town of Culdesac, interpreter; Tahtutash, a Nez Perce guide; and 50 men variously classified as laborers, cooks, teamsters, blacksmiths, and other workers.

They were well equipped with a plow, shovels, axes, wagons, tents, stoves, medicine chests, mess outfits, blankets, and food for 60 men for six months. All this cost about $20,000 leaving about $30,000 to be spent on the job.

They took the road to Pierce, going through Lapwai and over the Nez Perce Prairie, crossing the Clearwater River at Schultz's Ferry, now Greer.

In the meantime, Bird had gone ahead and scouted the area. The prospects for a road were anything but bright. There was six feet of snow in the mountains and the country was covered with a dense forest with heavy underbrush and plenty of windfalls. It was a dismal prospect, but Bird could not find any route that was better.

Bird then notified the Department of Interior that it was not possible to build a road through the mountains for $50,000. He said he would survey a route for a road and then attempt to build a trail on that location that could later be developed into a road. In the meantime, the Lewiston sponsors of the road would probably be less demanding.

Even a survey was difficult. The forests and brush were so dense that axe-men were required to open a line of sight. The country was steep and camping sites few and far between. The survey took a month. Bird arrived at the mouth of Lolo Creek in Montana on July 7 and his party was utterly exhausted.

Bird then returned to his construction crew over the Lolo Trail, but just to make sure that he was not overlooking a better route he sent George Nicholson, Major Truax, and Tahtutash over the southern Nez Perce Trail. They made the trip from Fort Owen to Elk City in eight days, which was something of a record for that time. Nicholson reported that the Lolo Trail was the better route.

Sometimes we see statements that the southern Nez Perce Trail was an easier route than the northern Lolo Trail. Actually, both routes were very difficult and, either way, a traveler would likely wish he had taken the other. One thing that may have confused people is that the Forest Service later completely relocated the southern Nez Perce Trail. Later the Forest Service trail was replaced by a motor way. Many people mistake segments of the Forest Service Trail as parts of the old southern Nez Perce Trail.

While Bird and his surveyors were locating a trail across the mountains, his crew widened the trail from Weippe to Musselshell into a road and moved to Musselshell. A large part of this road is on the same location as the road today.

The party spent the months of August and September in build-

*One hunting camp on the Lolo Trail distinguished itself
with a mailbox and an ironic address: 30-06 Lolo Trail.*

ing the Lolo Trail. Several important changes were made in the trail as followed by Lewis and Clark. Bird changed the trail from Indian Post Office to Indian Grave Lookout, following along the main divide. He also changed the trail from Sherman Saddle to Weippe. Instead of dropping into and climbing out of Hungry Creek he rerouted the trail along the main divide to Snowy Summit, thence to Musselshell, Brown's Creek, and Weippe. He graded from saddle to saddle, thus eliminating many steep sections and generally easing the grade.

The trail built by Bird was a very good trail. Trees did fall across it, and, since no one was responsible for keeping it open, it became clogged with windfalls. But its route remained practically unchanged from 1866 until it was replaced by a road in 1939, a period of seventy-three years. So the money was well spent.

In September, Bird realized that winter was near in the mountains. Eight thousand dollars remained of the appropriation. So Bird turned everything over to Major Truax and went to Washington. The Secretary of the Interior, knowing little about local conditions, was displeased that the project had been suspended and that Bird had taken it upon himself to appoint a successor.

The Idaho Territorial Legislature asked Congress for $60,000 to continue the project but Congress would not appropriate the money so the project came to an abrupt end.

Apparently the Bird construction crew named several features along the Lolo Trail. Snowy Summit, Rocky Ridge, Sherman Peak, Sherman Creek, Sherman Saddle, Noseeum Creek, Noseeum Meadows, Bald Mountain, and Indian Post Office are all names that apparently were first used by the Bird crew.

Chapter 8

CHIEF JOSEPH AND GENERAL HOWARD
The Nez Perce War of 1877

After the engagement between General Howard and Chief Joseph near Stites, the Indians retreated to Weippe. They arrived July 15, 1877.

In 1877 there were only a few ranches in the Weippe Prairie vicinity. They belonged to Patrick Gaffney, Martin Mouli, Peter Hourcade, Wellington (Duke) Landon, "Grasshopper" Jim Clark, and John Reed. These people fled to Pierce where a makeshift fortification was put together.

The Indians burned the ranchers' buildings, and, having lost a greater part of their food supplies at Stites, they proceeded to kill the ranchers' cattle and dry the meat.

The Indians held a war council. Some of the Indians, including Joseph, wanted to negotiate a peace treaty. Others, particularly those who thought they might be hanged for murder—and their friends—wanted to continue the fight. All the chiefs were convinced that they could not whip General Howard without assistance. They were faced with deciding whether they should negotiate a peace, flee to Canada, or seek aid from the Flathead or Crow Tribes, who had always been their friends. Finally, they decided to go to the Crow country and, if need be, later go to Canada. The Nez Perce, particularly Looking Glass, had always been on the friendliest terms with the white people in Montana and the Crows. They had every reason to believe they would

General Howard was a week behind the Nez Perce when he camped midway on the Lolo Trail in 1877.

experience no difficulty, a hope that led to bitter disappointment.

[Ethnographer Josiah Pinkham says that from time to time the Crow were adversaries of the Nez Perce. For more information, readers should consult *The Nez Perce Indians and the Opening of the Northwest* by Alvin Josephy, Jr.]

General Howard, after the battle near Stites, did not press the war. He did send out a scouting party that was ambushed. One friendly Nez Perce was killed near where the old trail from Kamiah to Weippe crossed Incendiary Creek.

It is not known just when Joseph and his band started over the Lolo Trail. They first moved to Musselshell Meadows. They were there when General Howard's scouting party was turned back. They then started over the Lolo Trail. Counting the days back from the passage around Fort Fizzle, it appears that they started on July 20 or 21 and were six days crossing to Graves Creek, a branch of Lolo Creek in Montana, arriving there on July 26.

Joseph's band consisted of about two hundred and fifty men,

about four hundred and fifty women and children, and two thousand horses. They followed the Lolo Trail as improved by Bird and Truax. But apparently the windfalls had not been removed since Bird did his work in 1866. The trail was choked with fallen timber. The Indians jammed their horses along, breaking legs and leaving the crippled and dying animals on the trail.

According to the Indians, the main party camped at Graves Creek Meadows.

There was ample horse feed and a trail leading to the Clark Fork River near Alberton if necessary to avoid the U.S. Army blockade at Fort Fizzle. Some of the warriors camped at Woodman Creek, where they could watch Captain Rawn build a log barricade a short distance down Lolo Creek.

The Indians camped at Graves Creek July 27 while their chiefs negotiated with Captain Rawn.

On July 28 the Indians bypassed Fort Fizzle. The women, children, and stock went up a ridge, then along the top of the divide, crossing down into Sleeman Creek, on the ridge between its forks, reaching Lolo Creek at the mouth of Sleeman about two miles above Lolo, Montana.

The warriors took a shorter route on the side-hill a short distance above the fort. They even fired a few shots at the fort to make sure the occupants stayed there while they passed by.

Where was General Howard on July 28? He was still at Kamiah, a fact that some people overlook when they write that General Howard was in hot pursuit of Joseph over the Lolo Trail.

Howard left Weippe, he called it Oy-ipe, on July 31. He camped that evening at Musselshell Meadows. Joseph was then leisurely moving south, up the Bitterroot River.

On August 1, Howard camped, I believe, at Soldiers Meadows, a small opening near Snowy Summit. There is water and feed there, what was left by the Nez Perce horses.

Apparently Howard reached Weitas Meadows on August 2. This is a good campsite. Here his trail-clearing crew, which had been recruited in Lewiston but which he had not waited for, overtook him. An officer's sword, now in the Clearwater Historical Society Museum, was found here.

On August 3, he apparently reached Bald Mountain, which has excellent horsefeed and water. A small number of cannon balls were left here. The Clearwater Historical Society Museum has one of these balls and a bayonet found on Bald Mountain.

On August 4, Howard reached what is now called Camp Howard. Here he received a request, by messenger, from Captain Rawn for assistance as he was following Chief Joseph up the Bitterroot Valley. Some cannon balls were also left at this camp.

August 5: Howard took his cavalry and went ahead. He camped where the Lolo Trail crosses Crooked Fork. This spot is heavily timbered. The horses had no feed.

August 6: Howard moved to Packer Meadows for breakfast, where an hour was spent eating and grazing the horses. He called Packer Meadows "Summit Prairie." He then went on to Lolo Hot Springs to camp.

August 7: Howard reached Lolo, Montana. His foot soldiers followed three or four days later.

With the crossing of the Lolo Trail, Howard's pursuit of Joseph had just started.

Howard had a cannon or maybe more than one. From Howard's accounts it is known that he used cannons against the Indians in the Clearwater Battle near Stites. Howard called these cannons Howitzers. They fired a ball about two inches in diameter.

There is a legend that Howard abandoned one of these cannon somewhere along the Lolo Trail. Various stories are told. Some say it rolled down the mountain from the trail and was abandoned. Others say it was buried in a rockslide. The location varies. The first report I heard was in 1924 when I was camped at Bald Mountain. The cannon was supposed to have been abandoned there, perhaps buried. I spent considerable time evenings and Sundays looking for it and prospecting likely looking mounds by driving a telephone ground rod into them, but I had no luck.

Later rumors placed the cannon somewhere in the vicinity of Rocky Ridge. The ground around there was thoroughly searched without success. The War Department insists that no cannon was abandoned. Nevertheless, the story persists that there is a cannon along the Lolo Trail. Frequently, someone reports that a certain person knows where it is, but when that person is approached he is surprised. He may, in turn, tell of someone else, living or dead, who knew all about it.

Early Forest Service employees Allen Space, A. N. Cochrell, Wilfred Renshaw, and others saw the cannon balls abandoned at Bald Mountain and at Camp Howard.

My brother Allen saw these cannon balls in 1918 but says by 1920 they had all disappeared. I camped at both sites in 1924, and they were gone by that time. A party from the University of Idaho went over the Lolo Trail in 1920. Forest Service employees believed that this party took the cannon balls with them. Why they took them and where is a mystery.

In 1928, a Mr. DeCray, a forest telephone lineman, found a cannon ball on Bald Mountain and the Clearwater Historical Society has one kept by Charles Meyers and Walter Sewell, but so far as I know, these are the only ones known today.

Chapter 9

THE CARLIN PARTY
A Tragic Hunt

In the middle of September 1893, three young men who had been planning a hunting trip for at least two years assembled in Spokane. They were William P. Carlin, the 27-year-old son of Brigadier General Carlin of Vancouver, A.L.A. Himmelwright, 28, an engineer, and John Harvey Pierce, 30, Carlin's brother-in-law from White Plains, New York. Carlin was considered the head of the party and had made some advanced inquiries about hunting places and conditions[17].

They decided it was too late to hunt for mountain sheep, but Carlin had talked to a guide, Martin C. Spencer, about an elk hunting trip into the back country of the Clearwater. Carlin had also made arrangements for George Colgate, 52, from Post Falls, Idaho, to go along as cook. Spencer at first objected to a man as old as Colgate going, but since he had cooked for Carlin before and Carlin insisted, Spencer finally consented. Of course, it should have been up to the guide, who knew the hazards of the journey, to make all decisions concerning safety of the party.

In Spokane they assembled an outfit of ten horses, guns, cameras, three dogs, and what appeared to be ample food supplies. This they shipped by railroad to Kendrick, Idaho, which was the nearest railroad depot to the Clearwater country in 1893.

On September 18, they left Kendrick and rode to Snell's Mill, or the present town of Cavendish, where Mr. Snell let them sleep in his barn.

They went over the Wheeler Ferry at Ahsahka on September 19, where the town of Orofino now lies, and on up the road to the top of the grade in the Fraser country.

By noon of September 20 they were at Weippe and purchased a sack of potatoes from Patrick Gaffney, who was concerned about their safety and warned them they should get out of the hills at the first sign of foul weather. They then went on to Brown's Creek, where due to rain they camped in a cabin.

On September 21 it was raining hard, so the party stayed at Brown's Creek, where they caught a string of fifty-three trout and killed four ruffed grouse. In the afternoon a rancher visited them. In a story of the trip Himmelwright published in 1895, he pokes fun at this rancher, but apparently he was a real mountaineer. He told them "I reckon you'll have a hard time in the snow, so late in the fall." He also told them, "It's a pretty tough trip for tenderfeet. Do you fellers all think you can stand the trip?" Likely he had his eyes on Colgate's gray hair and was in his way hinting that he should not go. The party resented his remarks and disregarded the warning.

On September 22 the party started over the Lolo Trail. They camped at Snowy Summit in about eight inches of snow, which should have been a warning to them that winter was close at hand.

The journey of September 23 was very difficult. The trail had not been cleared of windfalls since General Howard went over it sixteen years past. They camped at Weitas Meadows in five inches of snow. They had killed seventeen grouse that day and caught a string of fish at the meadows.

The journey of September 24 was even worse than the day before. The descent into the deep saddles and the climb out was exhausting. The windfalls were so bad the horses cut their legs and left blood on the snow. They camped at Bald Mountain. It was a clear night.

On September 25 they continued the journey and camped near Indian Post Office. It was a clear day.

Several hot springs attract winter visitors to the area along the Lochsa River where Jerry Johnson lived.

On September 26 they descended to the Lochsa River by the old trail, which has been partially replaced by the road to Jerry Johnson Lookout Point. When they reached the Lochsa, Colgate was exhausted, and his feet and legs were swollen. He insisted he would be all right with a day or two of rest.

The party was surprised to find a party of four camped there. Jerry Johnson and a prospector, Ben Keeley, were planning to stay all winter. They were building a cabin. The other two were hunters who had killed an elk and were preparing to leave for Missoula, which they did the next day. Jerry Johnson advised the party to make their stay short because of possible snow, but they thought Johnson wanted the hunting for himself.

In most stories, Jerry Johnson is pictured as something of a grouch. I talked with people who knew Jerry after he was too old to prospect and they say he was actually a rather jovial man. Apparently he was a little roiled at the Carlin party for not taking his advice. He could foresee the danger ahead and certainly wasn't going to do anything that would prolong their stay.

The hunt, if it could be called that, started the next day. It consisted of sneaking up on the licks at what are now called Jerry Johnson and Colgate Warm Springs and shooting at game there. They did not go out into the woods to hunt. They shot two elk but their shooting was poor. It required five or six gut shots before they could bring an animal down. They wounded a grizzly, but luckily it did not charge. The weather was miserable. It rained every day.

As it continued to rain, Spencer warned them they might get snowed in, but no one took his warning seriously. The cook, Colgate, continued to get worse. On questioning him, they learned that he had extreme difficulty in urinating. He had used a catheter for some time but neglected to bring it along. He was relieved of his work, but there was no feeling that it was urgent to get Colgate to a doctor.

On October 2 Colgate was in worse condition, and Spencer, their guide, urged that the party get out immediately. Pierce agreed with Spencer, but the others had not had enough hunting, and they hoped for better weather.

It continued to rain and by October 6 Colgate's legs had swollen to nearly twice their normal size and he was barely able to move without assistance. Spencer strongly urged that the party move out, but the party would not go.

On October 10 six inches of snow fell in their camp and more in the mountains. They then decided to move but ran into three feet of snow on the ridge above camp. They were trapped! The gates had been silently, softly, and firmly closed by coming winter.

The party now took stock of its situation. They had food supplies for eight days. Colgate was unable to walk. There was no possibility of getting through the Lolo Trail with horses. To travel it afoot pulling Colgate on a sled was an equally useless effort. The only way out was down the river, and that was not going to be easy. Spencer informed them that the river went through a very steep canyon.

They finally purchased Keeley's share of the food supplies and hired him to build rafts to take them down river. However, while Spencer helped Keeley finish the cabin, which took four days, the other members of the party continued to hunt. They killed two cows and a bull with the usual number of gut shots. They had plenty of meat. All they took of the bull was its hide and horns.

When the cabin was completed, Spencer and Keeley started on the rafts and had them ready to go on October 30. They did not get underway until November 3.

That day the party started down river but made only one mile when the larger raft tipped over in a rapid. They saved their food but all, including Colgate, were thoroughly soaked and cold.

The next day they took some of the stuff, including the precious antlers, back to Jerry Johnson. It rained hard all day, and Colgate was much worse.

On November 5 they started again and passed Indian Post Office Creek about noon after considerable difficulty. They camped on the first flat below Weir Creek, near the mouth of Ginger Creek. Here they noticed that the dogs kept sniffing the air as if game were near. Had they but known it, there is a warm springs a short distance up Weir Creek, and likely there were elk at the springs.

The battle with the river continued on November 6, but they made little progress. They camped on an island near the mouth of Ashpile Creek. They stayed there the next day to dry out and explore the country ahead.

The next day, Mr. Wright of Missoula, an experienced guide and friend of Spencer, sounded the alarm. He knew the conditions in the mountains.

Brigadier General Carlin organized relief parties. One party was to go in from Missoula and the other from the west. The rescue parties moved quickly, considering the transportation of the time. A rescue party under guidance of Wright left Missoula on November 10 and another coming from the west reached Weippe on November 13.

In the days that followed, Wright penetrated from the east as far as the old trail that climbs the ridge toward Rocky Point. Here he ran into four feet of snow and was forced to turn back.

Lieutenants Elliott and Overton arrived at Weippe, where they consulted the Gaffney family. Pat Gaffney had been in the Pierce-Weippe locality since the gold rush to Pierce in the 1860s. John Gaffney, one of his sons, was born near Pierce in 1868 and was raised in that locality. They were real woodsmen and mountaineers.

The Gaffneys advised them that to cross the Lolo Trail was next to impossible. They said that, although it would be rough going, it might be possible to travel up the Lochsa River. Furthermore, they reasoned, if the Carlin party was on its way out, it would of necessity come down the Lochsa river.

The rescue party split. Overton's party, with John Gaffney as guide, was to attempt the Lolo Trail, while the Elliott party, with Winn as guide, was to go to Kamiah and up the river. The next day, November 14, Elliott set out for Kamiah and Overton took the Lolo Trail.

Overton's party reached Snowy Summit, where it found snow so deep that the men could make only about a half mile a day. They were still fighting the snow when they received word that the Carlin party was found.

Now let us return to the Carlin party.

The party made good progress on November 8 for about five miles and camped near Skookum Creek.

The next day was a very difficult day. The rapids were terrible. They made about one mile and camped on the south side of the river near Holly Creek.

They made no progress November 10, 11, and 12. They scouted the river ahead and decided to abandon the raft. They also abandoned their companion, Colgate, and began to walk down the river. Accord-

The Carlin Party had to escape before the Lochsa River froze over, which generally occurs by the end of December.

ing to Himmelwright, Colgate was so far gone that he did not realize what was happening.

It took them until 1 p.m. on November 13 to cross the river, which they accomplished by falling a large pine tree. In the afternoon they crossed Bald Mountain Creek at about two miles and camped a half mile below.

On November 14 they made about five miles and camped near Noseeum Creek.

On November 15 they passed Boulder Creek about noon and camped at the present Lochsa Guard Center. Boulder Creek was named before 1893.

On November 16 it was necessary to fall a tree across Fish Creek for a foot-log. They called it Wild Creek. They camped at the upper end of the dreaded Black Canyon. In his diary Carlin stated: "The view did not impress me so much with its grandeur as with the undefinable dread weirdness. It immediately associated itself in my mind with death." They tried fishing, but the fish were so large they broke their hooks. They did succeed in landing three fish.

A determined assault was made on the canyon November 17, but they made only two and a half miles. At their campsite they found a copy of last summer's *Spokane Review*, which gave them courage.

On November 18 they climbed up and down cliffs all day. They made one and a half miles and camped a few yards east of Tumble Creek, about fifteen hundred feet above the river. They killed one grouse and had a difficult night. They left a gun there. So far as I know it has never been found.

About 4 p.m. on November 19 they reached the end of Black Canyon, and they camped near the mouth of Tick Creek.

On November 20 they ate the last of their food for breakfast and set out. They were growing weak and stumbled and fell a great deal but made progress and camped at Apgar Creek. They caught a one-pound fish for supper.

The next day they caught three fish for breakfast. They started out at 11 a.m. and made one mile, then came to a fishing hole at the mouth of Canyon Creek, where they camped and caught six large trout, which gave them a good supper.

On November 22 fishing failed to produce any food, and they started without breakfast. They met Elliott's rescue party, which was starting to portage the Hellgate Rapids, a particularly bad rapid at the mouth of Hellgate Creek.

Elliott wanted to go after Colgate but after learning how far it was, Colgate's condition, and the impassible state of the river above them, decided his efforts would be in vain. He dispatched a messenger to inform the other rescue parties and the outside world that the Carlin party was found.

He then took the party down river by raft to Ahsahka and by horse to Kendrick where they ate Thanksgiving Day dinner on November 30.

When the Carlin party reached safety, the news first caused a wave of rejoicing. But when it became known that they had abandoned Colgate without food or gun, the public turned on them in blazing anger. Every paper in the West criticized the party for violating the woodsman's creed that all must stick together regardless of circumstances. Charges and denials flew between Sanders, Keeley, and the Carlins. The truth could not be determined.

The Carlins paid Mrs. Colgate $25. The people of Post Falls held a meeting and collected money for the support of Colgate's widow and seven children.

Since Colgate was a Mason, that organization came to their assistance.

In February 1894, Colgate's son Charles and three other men went upriver in an attempt to find Colgate. They claimed to have gone up the river sixty-five miles, which would have put them to about Indian Grave Creek and well above where Colgate and the raft were abandoned. They found no trace of Colgate nor did they find the raft, which no doubt was where it had been abandoned. A tree, which they had set afire at one of the camps, fell and broke the collar bones of one of the party. The others helped him downstream to Pete King's place.

The next spring Carlin hired Spencer and two other men to search for Colgate. They brought out the hunting trophies but did not find Colgate. At the camp where he was abandoned they found evidence that Colgate had not left camp and high water in the spring runoff had flooded the site.

In midsummer, Lieutenant Elliott and party went into the Lochsa and traveled downstream to where Colgate was abandoned. They carefully searched below this point and eight miles farther down they found some of Colgate's bones, clothes, and small possessions. Elliott packed the remains up to Colgate Warm Springs and buried them. He placed some stones on the grave and set a post on which was burned "George Colgate."

The grave is now marked by a Forest Service marker and is a few feet below Highway 12 just east of Colgate Warm Springs.

Chapter 10

INDIAN GRAVE
A Death on the Trail

There is a small meadow and a spring in Section 1, T. 36 N., R. 10 E. along the old Lolo Trail. It is off the present Lolo Motorway and to the west of the road to Indian Grave Lookout. This is called Indian Grave Camp because of an Indian grave at the edge of the meadow. [Publisher's note: Indian Grave is along the trail from the Sinque Hole to Smoking Place, as mentioned on page 72.]

Some newspapers say this grave is that of a member of the Spalding family. But the Parsons family claims it is the grave of Albert Parsons, a cousin of William Parsons of Kooskia, brother to Jimmy.

Their account of the tragedy is that the family arrived at this camp late in the evening and prepared a hasty meal. The next day, every member of the family became seriously ill. Several family members came close to death, and Albert Parsons died. What caused the illness is unknown, but Jimmy Parsons, many years later, recalled what happened and concluded that food poisoning was the likely cause.

There is some confusion what year it was. The tombstone states that Albert Parsons was born in 1881 and died at the age of 14, which would make his death in 1895. This is the information I used in my book, *The History of the Clearwater National Forest.* However, a map prepared in 1894 by Lieutenant Elliott shows the grave. In discussing this inconsistent fact with William Parsons, he said that the birth date was correct and taken from written records, but the date of death was supplied by memory and could be wrong. Culby Mooers, an old pioneer and early day Forest Service packer, told me that the death occurred in 1892, but this also is memory.

The boy was buried near the meadow. A headstone without letters was placed at the grave. After the fire of 1910, the Forest Service placed a pole cover over the grave. About 1935 this pole covering became so decayed that it started to fall apart, so the Forest Service replaced the cover. By 1959 the second cover began to fall apart and in 1960 William Parsons marked the grave with a tombstone.

The name on the tombstone is Albert Parsons Mallickan. *Mallickan* was his Indian name and was an old Indian family name in the Kamiah and Kooskia locality. In the early days Nez Perce Indians frequently had both Indian and English names.

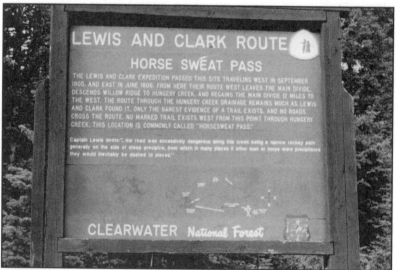

Way back in 1939, the U.S. Forest Service began installing historical signs like this on the Lolo Trail.

Chapter 11

THE FOREST SERVICE
Development of the Lolo Trail

In 1897, President Grover Cleveland proclaimed the Bitterroot Forest Reserve. It included territory in both Idaho and Montana. The Lolo Trail fell within its boundaries. Ten years later, after a number of changes, the Lolo Trail fell within the boundaries of the Lolo and Clearwater National Forests, where it has remained ever since.

In 1907 the Clearwater and Lolo National Forests received allotments for opening the Lolo Trail. They started from both ends. Work crews from the Lolo National Forest started at Lolo Hot Springs, which was the end of the road in Montana. Dwight L. Beatty supervised the work on the Lolo, and I am not sure but I believe he was the Ranger.

The work on the Clearwater National Forest was under the direction of Forest Ranger John Durant[18]. He spent considerable time on the job himself, but he also hired Ralph Castle as foreman, Walter Sewell, cook, and Charley Adams, packer. There were a number of axe-men and sawyers in the crew. They started out in May and moved to a small creek on the old road built by my father, C. W. Space, in 1897 or 1898 to take machinery to the old Pioneer Mine. They established camp and were almost immediately subjected to a snowstorm. They named the creek Siberia Creek and so it is today.

From Siberia Creek they built an almost level trail to the forks of Lolo and Yousa Creeks, thereby eliminating a muddy section of the old trail that went down Lolo Creek and over a low hill to Musselshell Meadow.

107

From the forks of Lolo and Yousa they climbed to the trail built by Bird, and all they needed to do was remove the windfalls and brush that had accumulated in the thirty years since General Howard went over it. Of course, there was plenty to do, but it was much faster now that they did not have to dig a tread.

The clearing crews met near Indian Post Office in mid-August and, since some money was still available, the crew moved back to Bald Mountain and built a cabin.

Thereafter the Forest Service maintained the Lolo Trail annually, and there was little or no change until road construction started at Lolo Hot Springs in 1925 and reached Powell in 1928.

A single-track road with turnouts was started in 1930 and sections built from both ends each summer, the crews meeting in 1935. A celebration was held at Indian Grave to commemorate the event. This was, and much of it still is, a very rough, steep, and crooked road. For the benefit of the numerous parties I have guided over the Lolo Trail, I wrote a little jingle. It goes like this:

> This road is winding, crooked, and rough,
> But you can make it, if you are tough.
> God help your tires, God help your load,
> God bless the men who built this road.

In addition to building a motorway along the Lolo Trail, the Forest Service has located and put up signs at many of the points of historical interest. Elers Koch, at one time supervisor of the Lolo National Forest and later assistant regional forester in charge of timber management, did much to locate the campgrounds of Lewis and Clark. He worded the first signs that were installed in 1939 and took part in seeing that they were properly located.

When I became supervisor of the Clearwater National Forest, I revived the effort to locate the campsites of Lewis and Clark and other points of interest along the Lolo Trail. Practically all camps are located and many have historical markers. Some of the markers are not at the exact place where the events took place. These changes were generally due to the necessity of placing them at a location where turnouts could be installed for the safety of the people who stopped to read them.

Usually these signs are historically correct, but here and there little inaccuracies have crept in to dramatize the event. For instance, the Forest Service has named many of the camps of Lewis and Clark, a thing the agency rarely did. One camp is named Wolf Camp because Lewis killed a prairie wolf—actually a coyote—and they ate it as part of their supper.

The Forest Service has plans for further development of this historic trail. The present road is not adequate. They plan to rebuild it and install historical markers, side trails where needed, and turnouts. The part of the route followed by Lewis and Clark through the Hungry Creek area no longer has a trail. The Forest Service plans to make this area accessible by trail, but not by road. This will give the public the opportunity to travel a part of the route by car or, if people wish, they can travel by a trail similar, though much improved, over the one followed by the explorers.

[Publisher's Note: The Lolo Trail is a National Historic Landmark. In the thirty years since the author wrote this book, there have been few improvements to the road he calls the Lolo Motorway. The road is not built to modern engineering standards and, in places, is badly eroded.

During the Bicentennial of the Lewis and Clark Expedition, the Forest Service plans to restrict travel on the high elevation portions of the road to ten parties a day between July 1 and October 1. They will give travel permits based on a lottery system.

The Clearwater National Forest will announce the availability of permits in December and visitors will have two months to apply, noting their preferred dates of travel. A maximum of ten parties a day will be allowed on the Trail, and each party can have up to ten people and two full-size vehicles and up to ten horses, mountain bikes, all-terrain vehicles, or motorcycles.

The Forest Service will issue one permit a week to institutions or organizations planning trips or special events on the Lolo Trail. These permits will allow up to thirty-five people and up to four vehicles.

For more information, please see page 131 of this book.]

A modern highway and well-maintained bridges make it relatively easy to travel in the Lochsa River Canyon today.

Chapter 12

THE NIGHTMARE
A Strenuous Experience

In 1924 I was running a crew for the Forest Service along the Lolo Trail. We were mapping the burns, correcting the map when we found errors, and taking sample plots in the stands of merchantable timber to get some idea of how much timber the area had and where it was located.

There were four of us in the party. Three of us—Frank "Red" Kouba, Charlie Fox, and I—did the mapping. Ed Nelson moved camp, looked after the stock, and did a major part of the cooking. We would stay in each camp about five days.

To move and supply camp we had a pack string of a saddle horse and six mules. One of the mules in this string—we called him Raspberry—was the meanest mule I have ever seen. He was strong, active, and dangerous. He never tried to throw a load off but anytime anyone was near him, that person had better stay on guard.

Besides being dangerous, this mule would not stay around camp. He was constantly running away, and the packer would have to hunt him up and bring him back. To save time hunting for this critter, the packer took to hobbling him.

We were camped at Camp Howard in mid-July, and one morning Ed Nelson was putting the hobbles on Raspberry. He had one end of the hobble on and was starting to put the other on, when the mule suddenly bashed out at Ed, striking and breaking his leg at the knee.

We improvised a stretcher and in a short time had Ed in bed. We then considered what we could and should do. First it was necessary to get word to the Ranger that we were in trouble and, if possible, get some help. We needed a doctor and more manpower if we were to get Ed out.

The nearest telephone was at Horseshoe Lake Lookout, about four miles away. So I left for the Lookout leaving Fox and Kouba to take care of Nelson. On arriving at the Lookout, I found two men, Harry Hunt and another man. I am not sure of the other man's name, but I believe it was Howell. I cabled the Lochsa Ranger Station at Boulder Creek and told them what had happened and that we needed help. Harry Hunt called his Ranger, Albert Cochrell, and was told to help us out the best he could.

Harry Hunt and I returned to camp. On the way there we discussed the best route and method to take Nelson to the end of a road. It was a long way in any direction. That is, we could go to Lolo Hot Springs, Montana, to Musselshell out of Weippe, or to the end of the road up the Lochsa, which at that time was at the mouth of Deadman Creek. We decided to take the latter route, not because it was much shorter, but because there were stations where we could stop overnight. It was about fifty-five miles. We decided that—if possible—we would arrange some method for putting our patient on a horse.

Next, we went about setting Ed's leg. I split out some rough boards and Harry Hunt shaped them to fit Ed's leg, using a butcher knife and his jackknife. He was very good at this. When we had everything ready, we set the leg. This is a terribly painful process, and we didn't have as much as an aspirin to give Ed.

We anchored his body by means of a rope around his chest under his arms, tied to a tree. We then tied another rope around his ankle and attached this to a lever. We then pulled hard and steady on the lever. We expected Ed to scream and steeled ourselves not to stop after we started pulling. Of course, Ed knew what was going to happen and, although he groaned, he did not yell. It took a pull of about ten minutes before the bone went into place, but it seemed like an hour.

I thought Ed fainted. He said he did not, but he was white as a sheet when we were through. The doctor later commended us on the good job we did.

As soon as the leg was set and splinted, Ed felt much better and said he believed he could ride a horse. We got the horse. He and the mule had been tied to a tree all day. I turned the mule loose, but I didn't take the hobble off, which was buckled around one foot.

When we tried it out, we found that Ed could not ride the horse. We then considered making a travois modified so that a man could carry the rear end of the poles, but our stock had never been broken to such a device. They were not gentle enough for us to try it without spending time training a horse or a mule. We decided that we would have to carry our patient on a stretcher.

We made a stretcher out of poles and canvas Manties. We trimmed away all excess wood to make it light as possible and rigged harnesses to go from the handles up over our shoulders so that the weight would not be entirely on our hands and arms. We then got everything ready for the next day's trip. We decided to take only our personal belongings, bedding, and a lunch. Our other camping equipment and food we would leave in a tent.

The next morning dawned cloudy and cool. Fox and Hunt cooked and washed dishes. Kouba brought the stock to camp. I cargoed our packs for loading. I cargoed Raspberry's saddle. I didn't want to fool with a mean mule. Oh yes! he was there. When he started to run, the hobble chain whipped him around the legs so he walked slowly and was too smart to run off with such a device.

After breakfast we loaded and were on our way, and such a way. We estimated we were carrying a load of about two hundred pounds. The man at Ed's head, since the shoulders of a man are heavier, was carrying about one hundred and twenty-five pounds and the other about seventy-five. Two would carry and two rest and one of the men resting would lead the pack string. It was strenuous work, and we had to stop frequently so everyone could rest.

The first half-mile out of Camp Howard was up hill and not bad going. We then went down the long grade to Saddle Camp. Just before we reached this place, a man from Castle Butte joined us. I have forgotten his name. He was a good worker and a big help.

We rested at Saddle Camp before starting the two-and-a-half-mile climb to Indian Grave Peak, a climb of about a thousand feet in elevation. Just before we started, it began to rain, and the trail was soon slick and the footing poor. We covered Ed with a canvas but we could not keep out all the water. It took us about two hours of backbreaking toil to reach the top. When we got there, the rain at the higher elevation had turned to sloppy snow.

I sent Hunt ahead to Indian Grave to build a fire, and we stopped there long enough to eat our lunches. We had come about seven miles in five hours. We had nine more to go.

After eating a hasty meal, we started on and we went about a mile when we met a man named Calhoun and Dr. Bryan from Kamiah. They each had a horse, and Calhoun was leading a mule with the Doctor's equipment. They had ridden part of the day before, most of the night, and reached us about 2 P.M. Calhoun joined in helping carry the stretcher, and a strong man helped a lot.

About 6 P.M. we reached the foot of Castle Butte, with one mile to go. Its top loomed five hundred feet above us, through the half rain and snow, mixed with fog. Here Fox became so exhausted that he just sat down and cried. He was only twenty years old and weighed about a hundred-forty pounds, so it was small wonder the work overcame him. I had him get on a horse and told him and the Doctor to go on ahead and get ready to receive the patient. I told them to tell Bert Botts to get started on supper. By this time Ed was so wet and cold he was shivering, and the Doctor feared he might get pneumonia.

We then picked up our patient and in about forty-five minutes arrived at the old Castle Butte Cabin. The doctor was ready. We took Ed into the cabin where the doc—as we called him—took off Ed's clothes, dried him off with a towel, and put him to bed. The doctor and Calhoun had brought slickers [raincoats]. The rest of us were sopping wet and had to change clothes. Hunt had no extra clothes, but

The author and his companions packed the injured man on a shoulder-mounted stretcher through the thick lodgepole pine.

Bert Botts fixed him up. Bert had supper ready, and we all ate heartily. Bert remarked that the station was not supplied well enough to feed such a hungry crew very long, but we were welcome to it as long as it lasted.

After supper I held a little get-together with the doctor and the crew. Ed was asleep. I think the doctor gave him a pill. I pointed out that the crew was exhausted. My hands and shoulders were blistered and sore, and every muscle in my body ached. I was no better off than the others. We still had thirty-eight miles to go. If we rested a day, we could probably carry Ed to the Boulder Ranger Station in one day. At that time there was no trail down the Lochsa River, so it would be necessary to go out over McLendon Butte, a raise of thirty-five hundred feet in elevation. We just had to get this man on a horse or get a lot more help. The latter would, of course, require considerable time.

The doctor assured us that he had all the plaster of Paris and other equipment to put Ed's leg in a cast as stiff as a board. If we could fix up a rig for supporting the leg, we could put him on a horse. We decided we could do this and would spend the next day at Castle Butte resting and putting Ed's leg in a cast. I assigned jobs to the men for the next day. Bert Botts and his partner were to take care of the wood supply and feeding the crew, Calhoun take care of the stock. Kouba and Fox would dry out our clothes and equipment, while Hunt and I fixed a rig for putting Ed on a horse.

It quit raining, and we prepared for the night. We were short of bedding, since Hunt, Calhoun, and the doctor had no beds. The blankets we used to cover Ed during our march were wet. We divided the bedding and canvass up the best we could. I slept under a wood shed and I really slept.

Bang! I awoke. That a shot was fired did not surprise me. Quite often crews were awakened by a shot, and there were plenty of pistols in camp, since four or five men had them. I stretched my sore muscles and put on my shoes. Due to the bedding shortage, I had slept with the rest of my clothes on. Then I got to thinking that the shot came from the direction of the corral. So I sauntered over that way, and there was the man from Castle Butte dragging a deer out through the woods. Apparently a deer had come to lick on the salt at the corral and had met his end.

Now, killing a deer out of season was strictly forbidden by the Forest Service, and anyone caught doing so would be fired. So I quietly turned around and without being seen went back to the cabin where we soon dined on Bert Bott's sourdough hotcakes.

After breakfast, we set about our jobs. Hunt and I set to work on a support for Ed's leg. We took some boxes apart for the boards and nails. We made a rig that was triangular in cross section. One side, carved to fit, rested against the horse and another for Ed's leg to rest on. We bored holes for ropes to attach it to the saddle, using hot spikes to drill the holes. In fact, our entire tool kit consisted of a hammer, saw, and jackknives, but that was enough.

About ten o'clock the sun came out and Calhoun asked me to help him take the hobble off Raspberry. I went with him to the corral. He caught Raspberry and tied him to the corral fence. He got on his horse and crowded Raspberry against the fence, while I reached under the lower rail and removed the hobble. We thought Raspberry would take off for parts unknown, but he followed us all the way to Pete King Ranger Station.

At supper, Botts placed a plate of steaks on the table with the invitation to "have some mutton." The only one to say anything was Kouba. He had never seen or eaten venison, but, being from Iowa, he had eaten plenty of mutton. He asked some questions but got no answers. Finally the doctor said, "Let me tell you about this mutton. Early this morning I went for a little walk, and I took Space's .45 along. It is a good thing I did because I was attacked by a sheep, and no sheep is going to bite me if I can help it." Of course, this wasn't an original story, nor was it told entirely for fun. The doctor was serving notice that he was taking responsibility for what had happened. If anything ever came of it, he was not responsible to the Forest Service. Those steaks were certainly good. Botts had to fry another skillet full.

The next day dawned bright and clear. We got underway about

6 A.M. We left the packing of our outfit to Calhoun and took just the doctor's and Ed's horses. Calhoun overtook us about three hours later.

We found that Ed could ride very nicely, but his foot stuck out so far there were places so close to trees that he couldn't get by. In that case it was necessary to take Ed off the horse, lead it past the tree, and then put him back on the horse. We soon worked out a system for doing this. It took four men besides the one who always led the horse. Two men stood on each side of the horse. Ed put his hands on the rear men's shoulders, usually mine and Bert Botts', since we were the strongest. The other two men took Ed's legs. We lifted him up. The horse was led ahead, and we walked past the tree and put Ed back over the rear of the horse into the saddle. Sounds simple—and it would be on the level—but usually we were on a steep hillside. Travel was about two miles an hour. It was also hard work for Ed, but he never complained about anything. He cursed himself for getting so careless as to let a mule break his leg.

About four miles out of Boulder Ranger Station I sent Bert Botts ahead to get us some lunch. We arrived about 12 o'clock, having made twelve miles in six hours.

After eating and resting about an hour, we started the long climb out of the Lochsa Canyon. We encountered the same difficulties as in the morning, but we arrived at Fish Butte Lookout at about 8 P.M. We had made eleven miles in seven hours.

We had worked thirteen hours, and we were all tired, but not as tired as two days before. Everyone felt good for the end was in sight. Sure, we had fifteen miles to go, but it was almost all down hill. It wasn't knee high to the twenty-three miles we had just made. That included a drop and rise of over thirty-five hundred feet. We had it beat!

Next morning we had a little delay getting our stock together, but we reached the mouth of Deadman Creek and the road about 3 P.M. There were cars waiting that took us all to Pete King Ranger Station. This was a brief stop for Ed who was soon headed for the hospital in Lewiston, Idaho. I never saw him again. I heard that when he recovered he had a slight limp. I said goodbye to the Doctor and thanked him. He warned me not to get bit by a sheep. Apparently he had picked me as the deerslayer.

We returned to our job, and after the blisters were fairly well peeled from our hands and shoulders, we were talking about the trip one evening and Charley Smith, our new packer, remarked that later on in life we could look back on this event as we dreamed of our youth. Fox said, "Well, if I ever dream of this trip, it will be some time when I am having a nightmare."

Chapter 13

TRAVELING THE LOLO TRAIL
A Guide for Those Following the Trail

I first crossed the Lolo Trail in 1924. I have no idea how many times I have been over it in the past forty-six years. I have walked it, ridden on horseback, and traveled by car. I have slogged over it through the rain and mud, fought fires along it in summer heat, dust and drought, and faced its blinding snows. I have seen it change from a trail to a road and highway. I have seen a large part of the area it traversed change from a sea of snags following the disastrous fire of 1919 into a beautiful forest.

The Lolo Trail has exacted its measure of toil, pain, suffering, and death. Yet it is beautiful country with a lot of history. In fact so much history that in 1965 it was designated a National Historical Landmark. It can be traveled in safety and pleasure if the traveler takes the proper precautions. The following is written to assist anyone not acquainted with the country. I would like you to have a safe and enjoyable trip over this old trail.

The time of year to go is between July 15 and September 15. Sometimes the snow is melted and the road open by July 1, but I have known it on rare occasions to open as late as July 20. Anytime after October 1 the road can be closed by snow although I have known it to be open as late as November 1. Passage in the winter by snowmobile is for the experts only. You could get caught in a blizzard that would make travel impossible for a week.

Almost any type of car can make it over the road, but it is too steep and crooked for trailers [and recreational vehicles (RVs)]. The larger and more expensive cars are not recommended, but I once conducted a group over the Trail and among the cars was a Packard and the driver had no trouble. Gasoline is sold at Lolo, Lochsa Cabins [Lodge] near Powell on the east, and Weippe on the west. Since it is about one hundred miles of steep road and slow going, with possible side trips, the traveler is advised to start out with a full tank. Some take an extra five gallons of gas along.

You can drive over the Trail in one day, but to really enjoy the trip and study the history connected with it, at least two days are suggested. This will make it necessary to go equipped to camp out.

Each car must be equipped with an axe, shovel, and water bucket since these are required by the Forest Service. Of course you must take cooking and sleeping equipment and be dressed for cool nights.

If you plan on building a campfire, it may be necessary to obtain a campfire permit. If you do your cooking on a gasoline stove and build no campfire, you need not be concerned about a permit. But even if you do not cook on a campfire, one will add cheer in the evenings. To me, one of the pleasures of camping is the fellowship gained by a "bullfest" around a campfire after supper.

You may travel the Trail equally well either from the east or the west and can use these instructions by reversing the order. In this narrative we will start from the east. I suggest you obtain a map from the Forest Service and study it as you read these suggestions.

You can stay overnight at Missoula, Lolo, or Lolo Hot Springs, or, if you prefer camping, there is an improved campground at Lee and Clark Creeks.

Now let us start over the Lolo Trail.

Going up Lolo Creek on Highway 12, the Forest Service and the State Highway Department have installed historic signs at the various points of interest, such as Lewis and Clark's campgrounds and Fort Fizzle.

Lolo Hot Springs is a privately owned resort, with rooms, a

restaurant, and a natural hot water pool. It is a beautiful spot with a historic sign.

At Lolo Pass, the Forest Service has a visitor center to serve the traveling public. [The Forest Service hopes to open a new visitor and interpretive center on Lolo Pass in 2002.] You should stop here, look at the exhibits of the Forest Service and Park Service. You can look at the maps and the material relating to the National Forest and the historic Lolo Trail.

Packer Meadows is about a mile from Lolo Pass. It is one of the most beautiful meadows I have seen and is well worth your attention.

If you wish to go to Lewis and Clark's camp of September 13, 1805, leave the highway at Lolo Pass on the road to Packer Meadows, take the first road to the right and go about one and a half miles. The Lolo Trail is cut by this road and it is abandoned, so you will need to watch closely. It is worn deep into the earth. Take this trail back toward the Meadows, and you will come to an opening with a small spring running into Pack Creek. This is where Lewis and Clark camped. The Forest Service has a marker planned, but at present it as marked only with an iron post driven in the ground. [Publisher's note: There is a sign here for Glade Creek Campsite and a trail with a short hike to the site.]

When you leave the Lolo Pass area, go west on Highway 12, and you will come to the DeVoto Grove. This grove is dedicated to the famed writer and conservationist Bernard DeVoto. It was here that DeVoto camped while collecting material for his book, *The Journals of Lewis and Clark*, and to fulfill his request, his ashes were cast over this area.

Going on to Powell Ranger Station you will come to where Lewis and Clark camped on Sept. 14, 1805. Here you will find a busy ranger station with friendly people who will be glad to answer your questions about permits, conditions of the road, and weather forecasts. The campground of Lewis and Clark has a sign, and you will likely wish to walk to the Lochsa River bank and see the island and the clear-running stream.

There are improved campgrounds at Powel Ranger Station, and at the Lochsa Lodge there are cabins for rent and a restaurant, and you can buy gas. [Publisher's note: A fire destroyed the restaurant at Lochsa Lodge during the winter of 2001. The owners plan to rebuild so the Lodge should be a good place to buy last-minute supplies for a Lolo Trail outing. Wayne Fairchild, an outfitter, bases his Lewis and Clark Trail Adventures in a cabin at Lochsa Lodge.]

Four miles west of Powell on Highway 12 is Whitehouse Pond and Wendover Creek. This is the area Lewis and Clark called "the Fishery," and it was just west of Wendover Creek that Lewis and Clark left the Lochsa and made the difficult climb to the Lolo Divide on Sept. 15, 1805.

The Lolo Motorway—as I call it—is the road that closely follows the Lolo Trail and leaves Highway 12 a short distance east of the road to Powell Ranger Station. It climbs to the top of the ridge at Powell Junction. Watch your map and the signboards to make sure that you do not get off on some of the logging roads that are wider than the Lolo Motorway.

The Lolo Trail went through Powell Junction. You can still find it, and it was only a short distance west of Powell Junction on the south side of the mountain that Lewis and Clark camped on June 28, 1806.

The road forks at Powell Junction. The road to the east goes to Rocky Point Lookout. If you should go there, you can obtain a view of a beautiful country, and the lookout will be glad to point out points of interest.

The first point of interest when going west from Powell Junction is the Forest Service sign marking the trail Lewis and Clark took when they came up Wendover Ridge [to Snow Bank Camp].

Next you will come to the forks of the road at Cayuse Junction. This is one of Work's camps. If you should wish to camp near this locality, take the road north and, in about a half-mile, you will come to Cayuse Creek and a fair place to camp.

From Cayuse Junction, going west, you come to Spring Hill, which has a Forest Service marker.

Next you come to the road that goes to Jerry Johnson Lookout and the Lochsa River. This is the route Carlin took to the Lochsa River in 1893.

Going on west you come to Indian Post Office, the highest point on the Lolo Trail. Indian Post Office has a Forest Service sign.

Just west of Indian Post Office is a directional sign pointing toward Post Office Lakes. You cannot see the lakes from the road but a few steps will take you to the top of the ridge and you can look down on two beautiful lakes. Don't be fooled by how close they look and start down to the nearest lake unless you wish to spend several hours making the trip down and back up.

The next point of interest is Camp Howard. The road forks here. The northerly fork goes to Horseshoe Lake Lookout. If you take this fork, in about a quarter-mile you will come to a small creek and meadow. Here is where General Howard camped on Aug. 4, 1877. This is a good campsite, and many people have camped here. It is not marked nor is the campground improved.

About a mile west of Camp Howard is the Devil's Chair. This is a huge rock rising about 30 feet above the ground on the upper and about 100 feet on the downhill side. This rock has a smaller column on one end not quite as high as the main rock and the top of this small column is shaped like a huge easy chair. It is called the Devil's Chair because a person who climbs the main rock, which is not difficult, is tempted to jump down onto the chair. Then he is trapped, because only the best jumpers can jump back up and a miss would be fatal. Don't try it!

At Saddle Camp, a logging road crosses the Lolo Motorway. This is a good road and if you have had enough of the Lolo Motorway you can take this road and in a short time be back on Highway 12.

The Forest Service has a sign on the Lolo Motorway which states that the Sinque Hole Camp of Lewis and Clark on Sept. 17, 1805, is located above it. However, it is not easy to find this camp. The best way to reach it is to start from the first draw east of the Forest Service sign. Here, if you scout around above the road, you will find the old Lolo Trail. [Publisher's note: The old Trail is now well-marked with a

A person can easily jump down on the Devil's Chair but can't climb back up. The author says, "Don't try it!"

sign on the Lolo Motorway.] This should be followed westward to the top of the ridge. The sinque hole is on the Lochsa side of the ridge from where you reach the top. The old Lolo Trail is worn deep and has many windfalls across it.

There is a branch road that goes to Indian Grave Peak, which is a lookout station. Following up this road, you will come to a meadow. On a low rise across this meadow is the grave of Albert Parsons.

At the east side of this meadow there is a good place to camp, except in July when the mosquitoes are very bad.

The peak south of Indian Grave is where the Indians had Lewis and Clark stop and smoke. [There is now a marker here.]

Going west you come to the road to Castle Butte Lookout. From this peak you get a spectacular view of the Lochsa River about three thousand feet below. When I look down from this peak today, I marvel at the strength, endurance and agility of my youth when I walked from this peak to the River and back in one day just to prove the old map

125

which showed Castle Creek running into Holly Creek was in error. The area is burned over now and from the lookout it is obvious that these creeks do not join.

Bald Mountain is the next point west. The best place to camp is on the east end where there is a spring and a well-used camp spot under a spruce grove. From the camp area a trail leads on a gentle grade to Bald Mountain Lake, which is another beautiful spot. Bald Mountain is a famous camping site. Lewis and Clark, Work, Howard and Carlin camped there. Likely Joseph did. The signboard mentions only Lewis and Clark.

Three miles west of Bald Mountain is a sign marking the camp of Lewis on September 18, 1805.

Noseeum Meadows is a nice place to camp after about August 15. Before that date the mosquitoes and a black gnat, so small you can hardly see it—a "no-see-um"—is quite bad. The Nez Perce called this *We-wei-at-tep-ka*, which means many springs.

Sherman Peak is best climbed from the east side. You should go up the road west from Noseeum Meadows until you reach the point where the road starts downgrade. Park your car here and climb the mountain. It is a fairly steep climb and about a half-mile to the top. You will find parts of the old trail on the way up. From Sherman Peak you will observe the "Columbia Plains" as Lewis and Clark did in 1805. [Publisher's note: Today an improved Forest Service trail takes off from a Forest Service sign. The climb is on the west side now along a trail that switches back and forth across the slope all the way to Sherman Peak. Plan on a four-to-five hour climb.]

Sherman Saddle is where the trail followed by Lewis and Clark left the main divide. It angled south to the top of the ridge west of Sherman Saddle, and then dropped into Hungry Creek. It was on this ridge west of Sherman Peak that the "deposit" was made when the party returned to Weippe. There is a Forest Service sign. The Forest Service plans to reopen the old trail into Hungry Creek, but it will require time and money.

From Sherman Saddle west you are on a road that follows closely the trail built by Bird. It is also the route taken by Work, Howard, Joseph, and Carlin.

Weitas (originally "wet ass") Meadows are rather swampy and although people frequently camp there, I do not recommend it because the water is on the unsafe side. Likely Howard and Joseph camped here. So did Carlin.

If you wish to see another beautiful lake, take the short drive to Rocky Lake.

The road forks about three miles west of Rocky Ridge. The road that turns sharply to the north will take you to Musselshell and Weippe and is a much shorter road than the one to the south. There is a good place to camp at Camp Martin. This is the trail built by Bird, and at Camp Martin a piece of this old trail still leads past the spring and down to Lolo Creek.

The southerly route will take you back to the route followed by Lewis and Clark and if you wish to go to the Meadows where Clark killed the horse, take the road to Boundary Peak. When you come to a sign marked Windy Saddle you will find a trail leading north. If you go down this trail about one quarter mile, you will come to Hungry Creek and the meadow. There is no marker, although one is planned.

Returning to the forks of the road and going south, you will come to a good logging road that turns to the right and reaches Eldorado Creek at the mouth of Dollar Creek where Lewis and Clark camped and fought the mosquitoes. Going on down Eldorado Creek, you will pass the June 15 camp of Lewis and Clark at the lower end of the meadows. No marker at present.

When you come to the Cedar Creek road, go up it and you will come to the Lewis and Clark Grove where Clark camped on Sept. 19, 1805. This site has a Forest Service sign. While here, take a look at the large trees and especially the large white pine called the Clark Tree.

Now go back down Cedar Creek to Lolo Creek road and down it to "Wolf Camp," where Lewis camped on September 21, 1805.

If you follow the road on down Lolo Creek it will take you to Kamiah. If you go back up the Lolo Creek Road and follow the directional signs, you will come to Musselshell Meadow. This is the old campground of Joseph and Howard. The Forest Service has also had a ranger station or work center here since 1898.

If you are here about the middle of August, you can probably watch the Nez Perce Indians gathering camas and roasting it by the same process Lewis and Clark described.

From Musselshell it is about ten miles to Weippe. From Weippe west to Lewiston the only campsite of Lewis and Clark that is marked is at Canoe Camp on Highway 12. There is at present little development here, but it is a part of the Nez Perce National Historical Park system and will eventually be improved.

Kamiah and Orofino have accommodations for tourists.

Lewis and Clark Trail Adventures

An unexpected guest, Missoula actor Ritch Doyle, impersonates William Clark in an outfitter's camp along the Lolo Trail.

NOTES

1. In the author's original edition, the spelling was *Khusahnah Ishkit,* which was given him by Elizabeth Wilson of Kamiah. Nez Perce ethnographer Josiah Blackeagle Pinkham was kind enough to modernize the spelling to its current form, *Kuseyne 'Iskit.*

2. The author found evidence of Indian use of the following sites on the Lochsa River and Lolo Trail. Take the Lochsa River first:

Mouth of White Sand Creek—chips only.
Wendover—broken fish knife and chips.
Squaw Creek—a beautiful modern type arrowhead and chips. These were thrown out by road construction.
Mouth of Warm Springs Creek—another beautiful modern arrowhead, a musket ball, chips.
Island near mouth of Ginger Creek—stones for a sweathouse, broken artifacts.
One mile above Bald Mountain Creek—numerous chips, broken tool for making canoes, and ancient missile point, very old.
Just above Five Islands—a scraper, old.
Sherman Creek—chips, scraper, cooking stones, arrowheads, old and modern.
Fish Creek—numerous chips, a moderately old obsidian arrowhead.

The Lolo Trail:

Powell Junction—numerous chips and a large piece of obsidian, apparently lost in transit.
Saddle at head of Papoose Creek—a modern arrowhead made from basalt, chips. I searched around Indian Post Office but found nothing. A man in Lewiston once tore down one of the rock cairns there. He informs me he found nothing.
Place where Lewis and Clark stopped so Indians could smoke—chips. This area heavily sodded.
Bald Mountain—a copper ornament and a modern type scraper.
Noseeum Meadows—chips. This area is sodded over.
Sherman Peak—many chips, a knife, and a red chalcedony arrowhead, modern.

3. Josiah Blackeagle Pinkham, an ethnographer with the Nez Perce Tribe, believes the trail is much older than this. He says that while it is true to some extent that Indians used the rivers as a travel route, it is misleading to assume this was their preference over the Lolo Trail.

4. Archaeologist C. Milo McLeod, a forest archaeologist with the Lolo National Forest, has also concluded that it might not have been the case that the earlier trail followed the rivers and streams. Archaeologists have found artifacts on the ridge trail dating back before the Indians' acquisition of horses. And long, linear, interconnected ridge systems made sense because they avoided the brush-choked drainages and steep hillsides along the rivers. The high ridge trail was also faster because it didn't meander back and forth as did the rivers and streams.

5. Modern archaeological research suggests that game populations along the Lolo Trail ecosystem are cyclical and responsive to the variations of vegetation brought by fire. While it is true Lewis and Clark encountered little game in 1805 and 1806, big

game populations increased sharply after 1900. The major fires of 1910, 1919, 1929, and 1934 burned vast areas of deadfall and overly mature timber (Koch 1934:99). However, the areas quickly revegetated with a variety of grasses, shrubs, and brush, creating ideal browse habitat for many big game species.

6. Taken from General Howard's writings.

7. See *Journals of David Thompson* by Catherine White.

8. The author spent a great deal of time with Harry Wheeler when he was well. The author discussed many historical points with him to get the Nez Perce version, and they visited a number of historical sites together.

9. As stated by Josephy in an article concerning the Lolo Trail in the *Lewiston Tribune*. He had studied Work's map.

10. See the encyclopedia.

11. Himmelwright's map in book *In the Heart of the Bitterroot Mountains*.

12. Quotations are taken from Thwaites *Journals* and Sergeant Patrick Gass' diary.

13. *The Trail of Lewis and Clark* by 0. D. Wheeler, 1904.

14. According to Kate McBeth. Corbett Lawyer, an aged Nez Perce, told the author this story.

15. For more information about this remarkable leader, Nez Perce ethnographer Josaih Blackeagle Pinkham suggests the book *Hear Me My Chiefs* by L.V. McWhorter.

16. See summer issue of 1955 *Montana Magazine*. Josiah Pinkham says there is a photograph of Capt. Clark's son in existence.

17. This story of the Carlin party is based on *In the Heart of the Bitterroots* by Himmelwright, a member of the Carlin Party, plus interviews with Ed Gaffney, son of John Gaffney, from material by my father, and newspapers.

18. According to Walter Sewell.

19. The author was indebted to William Parsons of Kooskia for the spelling of Indian names.

20. The author was indebted to Marcus Ware of Lewiston and Mr. Harris of Lapwai for reviewing this book and making suggestions, and to his wife who did the typing.

AFTER 2002 YOU MUST APPLY FOR A U.S. FOREST SERVICE PERMIT

Because of the cultural and historical significance of the Lolo Trail, the Clearwater National Forest is implementing a permit system from July 1 to October 1 between the years 2003 and 2007. The Forest will announce the availability of permits in December for the following year and grant permits through a lottery system. Visitors will have two months to apply for their preferred dates of travel.

The permits will cost $6, and the Clearwater Forest will allow a maximum of ten parties on the Lolo Trail each day. Each party can have up to ten people and two full-size vehicles, and up to ten horses, bicycles, ATVs, or motorcycles (as long as the ATVs and motorcycles have noise abatement systems).

Organizations or institutions can also apply for permits to travel the Trail. They can have up to thirty-five people and four vehicles, but only one such large party will be allowed on the Trail each week. For more information, you can write or call:

BICENTENNIAL COORDINATOR
Kooskia Ranger Station
Route 1, Box 398
Kooskia, ID 83539
(208) 926-4274

OUTFITTERS LICENSED TO GUIDE THE LOLO TRAIL

TRIPLE "O" OUTFITTERS
Harlan and Barbara Opdahl
P.O. Box 217
Pierce, ID 83546
(206) 464-2349
Email: hbopdahl@clearwater.net

LEWIS & CLARK TRAIL ADVENTURES
Wayne and Gia Fairchild
P.O. Box 9051
Missoula, MT 59807
(406) 728-7609
Email: raft@montana.com

Please note that licensed outfitters are not subject to the permit system and that more outfitters may be licensed by the time of the Lewis and Clark Bicentennial in 2004. For an up-to-date list of licensed outfitters, contact:

IDAHO OUTFITTERS AND GUIDES LICENSING BOARD
Dean Sangrey
1365 North Orchard, Room 172
Boise, ID 83706
(208) 327-7380
Fax: (208) 327-7382
Email: dsangrey@oglb.state.id.us
http://www2.state.id.us/oglb/oglbhome.htm

OTHER RESOURCES ON THE INTERNET

The Clearwater National Forest
http://www.fs.fed.us/r1/clearwater/index.htm

Lewis and Clark National Historic Trail
http://www.nps.gov/lecl/

The Lewis and Clark Trail Heritage Foundation
http://www.lewisandclark.org/

State of Idaho
http://idptv.state.id.us/lc/index.html

Traveler's Rest Preservation Project
http://www.travelersrest.org/news/news.html

The Nez Perce Tribe
http://www.nezperce.org/

Lewis and Clark Historic Trail (Bus) Tours
http://www.rmdt.com

OTHER RESOURCES ON THE NEZ PERCE TRIBE

The Nez Perce Indians and the Opening of the Pacific Northwest by Alvin Josephy Jr.

Nez Perce Country, An Official National Park Handbook

Hear My Chiefs!: Nez Perce Legend and History by Luculus V. McWhorter

Yellow Wolf: His Own Story by Luculus V. McWhorter

A Little Bit of Wisdom: Conversations with a Nez Perce Elder by Horace P. Axtell

Salmon and His People: Fish and Fishing in Nez Perce Culture by Allen Pinkham Sr.

The Nez Perce Tribe
Cultural Resource Program
P.O. Box 365
Lapwai, ID 83540
(208) 843-7400

Nez Perce National Historical Park and Museum
Route 1, Box 100
Spalding, ID 83540
(208) 843-2261

Lewis and Clark Trail Adventures

One of the best ways to see the Lolo Trail is on bicycles.

INDEX